BOOKER T
&
THEM

BOOKER T & THEM

A BLUES

As presented by

BILL HARRIS

Wayne State University Press
Detroit

16 15 14 13 12   5 4 3 2 1

Library of Congress Cataloging-in-Publication Data

Harris, Bill, 1941–

Booker T. & them : a blues / as presented by Bill Harris.

p. cm. — (Made in Michigan writers series)

ISBN 978-0-8143-3716-5 (pbk. : alk. paper) —

ISBN 978-0-8143-3717-2 (e-book)

1. African Americans—Poetry. 2. United States—Race relations—History—Poetry. I. Title.

PS3558.A6415B66 2012

811'.54—dc23

2011031401

∞

Designed and typeset by Maya Rhodes
Composed in Walbaum LT and Duality

Contents

Preface

Imagine with me, if you will, what it was like to be a black person of note at the beginning of the twentieth century. The early 1900s was a (particularly) tough time for Negroes, famous or nameless. It was an era when the only acceptable answer to a question put to a person of color was what the white inquisitor wanted to hear. A response deemed, God or Jim Crow forbid, uppity, sassy, or contrary to the questioner's need to cling to the myth of superiority, could be capricious, unreasoned, or remorseless. The punishment could come in legislative, emotional, or physical form; it could well be worth one's life. To be black and have your name in a newspaper—not as a statistic in the lynched-this-week log—was, therefore, rare, but likely to subject you to verbal abuse with no compunction regarding its lack of fairness, human kindness, or justice.

Despite those givens a number of African Americans lifted their heads, straightened their spines, and rose to course-changing status as they spoke and acted in their various ways against the torrential current of the mainstream. My interest in this bio-poem, set during this so-called age of Booker T. Washington, is the depiction, in historical and imaginative ways, of several figures, with the emphasis on black males in the process of seeking to be men who mattered in a racist America. Also of concern are their effects on history and each other. Call it a gathering of evidence for a hoped-for greater understanding through the poetic route of who they were, and the forces that shaped them.

There are several invented characters—the students and professors of Tuskegee, for instance—whose creation and inclusion are in no way meant to alter the actual history of the period. They are simply aids in the telling of the story and the revelation of our subject characters. All quotes are accurate and from the individuals to whom they are attributed. The emphasis in *Booker T. & Them: A Blues* is literary. It is not meant to replicate my earlier visit to the period, nor to be guided or judged by the intentions of that effort.

It is therefore dedicated to those men, Booker T. Washington, W.E.B. Du Bois, William Monroe Trotter, Jack Johnson, George Washington Carver, the blues singers and ragtimers et al., who, defying the tremendous odds and realities against them, proved to be alchemists spinning the straw of improbability into the gold of seized opportunity, and mastered the art of being masters of their moments in time.

I'm using modes now, because I'm trying to get more form in the free form. Furthermore, I'd like to play something—like the beginning of "Ghosts"—that people can hum. And I want to play songs like I used to sing when I was real small—folk melodies that all the people will understand. I'd used those melodies as a start and have different simple melodies going in and out of a piece. From simple melody to complicated textures to simplicity again and then back to the more dense, the more complex sounds.

—**Albert Ayler,** Notes for "Complete Live at Slug's
Saloon Recordings," Lone Hill Jazz, 2004

Hum hm h*mummm*
2-3
Hum hm huum*mummm*

Which Treats the New Century in the New Nation & a Couple of Movers & Shakers Who Shake & Move It

". . . a people full of hope and aspiration
and good cheer."
Mark Twain,
"A Greeting from the 19th Century
to the 20th Century"

Changes. Speed. Land, sea, & air. Radio. Telegraph.
Telephone. Phonographs. Music. Film. Emigration.
Booker T. Washington.

Hear the oompa oompa oompa oompa
as the rich
get
richer,
the poor
need
more, time
& the Press & Church & State & the A-

merican pop-
ulace con-
sumers, the A-
mericanists,
Forward March, as the band
plays on.

"Give the public what it wants," is Edison's
Barnum-influenced creed. & still it is a tough
time for negroes.

Flicker:
In the beginning see 1900. See deep
darkness upon the face of the new century.
See the spirit of Edison, Thomas A. move.
Let there be light, Edison says, & there is . . .
& the lights see that it is good that the light
is still divided from the dark's formless void. &
the lights say let it continue to be: them
under, & us above: & it is so. & it
is good, & still it is a tough time for
negroes.

"I never did a day's work in my life. It was
all fun." Thomas A for Alva
Edison (1847–19-
31) tinkers, & is a man of
business. "I find out what the world needs. Then I go
ahead and try to invent it."

See the "Wizard of Menlo Park" at the "electric
Mecca." Operating on 3 hours' nightly sleep.
"To invent you need a good imagination
and a pile of junk."

Invents the light bulb + the electric

generator + the motion picture projector
+ the phonograph. "Of all my inventions, I
liked the phonograph best. . . ." + one thousand 89
patent-worthy others. He dreams of devising
a device to cross-circuit death's dark & formless
divide & converse with the late lamented lights
extinguished from one's life.

1900
Over There: the Sousa Band, the best (ho-hum) America has to of-
fer, "The most famous band of all time," their earlier scheduled trip
postponed by Theodore Roosevelt's set-to with the Spaniards over
some bully business in Cuba, march, through France, Germany,
England, Belgium, & Holland Oomphoomphoomph & boom-
boom-booming the gospel of American liberty & ratatattattat,
while Sibelius, Toulouse-Lautrec, Chekhov, Tolstoy, Renoir, Elgar,
Conrad, & Freud, with their shifts & changes, their sleights-of-
hand, their cultural & intellectual charge advancing tricks of light,
light a new way. Next year (sigh) Sousa'll load up & do it all over
again, two 3 four.

Over Here:
1900
Lynchings: 106 are on the books.
Census: Negroes @ a shade under 9 million
= 11.6% of the population.

Over There: Paris Expo World's Fair. U.S. pavilion. Assembled
works, signs, & symbols of self-improvement, by & about African
Americans, & photographs curated by W.E.B. Du Bois & his intel-
lectual Atlanta Historic Black College cronies of clean, *Exposition
des Negres d'Amerique,* "picturing their life and Development," Du
Bois says, "without apology or gloss."

Over here:
Tom E., home-schooled-whip-smart-killer-diller & ½

deaf, nose to the grindstone, hustler-bustler, says,
"There's a way to do it better—find it," "I start
where the last man left off."
                              Ear to the ground,
like the conjurers of blackened-faced minstrelsy,
or Buffalo Bill, or Barnum, listening for rumblings
of the public's cravings, while tinkering, with high-tech ways
to beat the time of man & beast
& call the tune
of fun for, &
profit from
the common folk.

"The thing with which I lose patience most is the clock.
Its hands move too fast."—T.A.E.

Re
Time, it is Booker T. Washington Time.
Some chroniclers call black history from 1881 to 1915
"The Age of Booker T. Washington."

See
Booker Taliaferro (originally
Tagliaferro, "iron cutter" in
Italian) Washington.

Born 1856, in the 4th year of
Franklin Pierce's one-term presidency.
The South-leaning New Englander acquires New
Mexico & Arizona & lets pro &
antislavers shed blood over land opening
in the West. Alcoholism, separation,
supporting the Confederacy,
& cirrhosis follow—for Pierce, that is.

Edison will, in time, make moving pictures
(often restaged) of 'most anything in motion.
Will make possible the performance without
the presence (or bother) of the performer.

He also produces *Ten Pickaninnies,*
a documentary. A litter of real but
more-pets-than-potential-people negro children
at play. Inky, smoky, & snowballs, the title cards
call them, coons, & little black lambs.

Booker T. will come up; build Tuskegee into
a machine. For 2 hundred years will be the most
powerful Negro raised in America.
A blues will be sung in his name.

& still it is a tough time for negroes.

Which Treats of the Station in Life & the Pursuits of the Famous Colored Gentleman, Booker T. Washington, & His Sally to Break Bread with President Theodore Roosevelt TR, & That Meal's Aftermath

1901
Scan Dixie.
See "Swamp State" (nee *Carolana*)–born "Pitchfork Ben"-
jamin Ryan Tillman, 1847–
1918. Once its governor (when
the population was 40.1% white & 59
.9 % black), & 4 times its senator.
Embodying the unrepentant supremacist
white attitude in post-Reconstruction,
the 1-eyed forefather of Clemson &
Winthrop Colleges speaks on disenfranchising
South Carolina's black citizens: "We have done

our level best . . . we have scratched our heads to find out
how we could eliminate the last one of them. We
stuffed ballot boxes. We shot them. We are not
ashamed of it," he crows from the first state to have
split from the Union.
                              See 406.6
miles north. The White House. Interior 2-shot:
see Booker T. Washington, Founder &
President of Tuskegee in Macon
County in the state of Alabama,
& Theodore Roosevelt, U.S.
President, only a month on the job, hosts
Washington who'd come to dinner. To "talk over
the question of possible appointments in the South."

"The President Dines a Darkie" & "President
Roosevelt Proposes to Coddle Descendants
of Ham" is the news fit to print. "Social
equality means decadence and damnation,"
Tillman bitches.

(57 years earlier
the guest roster lists the Command Performance
of The Ethiopian Serenaders,
a Blackface minstrelminstrel troupe, "for the Especial
Amusement of the President . . . [John Tyler—Whig,
supporter of state's rights & other Southern interests,
annexer of Texas, father of 15, &
expelled from his own party—1790–
1845], His Family and Friends . . .").

"The three great essentials to achieve anything
worth while are," Edison says, "first, hard work; second,
stick-to-itiveness; third, common sense."

16 October, 1901:
Picture Roosevelt & Washington: 2 soft-walking
performance artists who carry big shtick, jostling.
Washington, born a slave, is, in the anything-
is-possible 20th century, "The most
influential negro in America." The
Wizard. The Power broker. Accommodator.
Compromiser. Apologist. His Tuskegee
Institute Manual Arts Education Program
die-cuts dark drudges for the heavy lifting
industrial needs of his Robber Baron
benefactors.

     See Republican Roosevelt,
who Mark Twain says is "the most popular human . . .
that has ever existed in the United States"
(1858–1919, 26th
President), bespectacled, blind in one eye,
nearsighted in the other. A snobbish Swell
& once puny, sickly lad, played "store and baby,"
branded Punkin-Lily & Jane-Dandy. Who, as
a man, while grieving the same day deaths of wife &
mother, exiles himself to the Bad Lands. Masters
the frontier territory, its trials & trails. Re-
turns re-made; hardy, scrapper. Man's man. Maverick.
Hawk. Pot-bellied, bandy-legged Bully Boy puff.
Ascends like Zeus from Societal Olympus.
Enters the Arena of Politics. Is a
progressive regulator, reforming trustbuster,
an imperialistic gunboat diplomat.
A nationalist naturalist. Is robust.
Is full of himself. Is Veep at 42.
Youngest Pres ever at 42. Made so by
an anarchist assassin's .32. Is,
according to lawyer, lecturer, state
legislator, preacher, playwright, screenwriter,
actor, real-estate speculator, novelist

（9）

Thomas Dixon, "honest, patriotic,
intelligent and brave as a lion."
                    (More on
Dixon when time, space, & chronology permit.)

As president, Roosevelt (TR) packs a gat.
Is 1st chief-exec of the moving picture age.
As with the West he masters the medium. He
exudes dynamism, zing, vigor. The camera
loves him. Makes it his ally. The teddy bear will
(next year) be named for him. Thomas Edison's
motion picture short *Goldilocks & the Three Bears*
will be about TR. Roosevelt is "THE BEST
OF AMERICA." "You're All Right, Teddy," is his
1904 presidential campaign song penned
by colored brothers John Rosamond (18-
73–1954) & James
Weldon Johnson (1871–19-
38), educator, lawyer, &
secretary of the NAACP,
appointed (1906) by TR A-
merican consul to Venezuela &
Nicaragua, author, poet (*God's Trombones* &
"Lift Every Voice and Sing").

Johnson's 2-faced protagonist, "Ex-Colored man"
in *The Autobiography of an Ex-
Colored Man*, a novel, is mulatto. His
dilemma, face the public as a ragtime pianist,
or hide his dark side in middle class white obscurity?

Showing his full frontal whiteness TR says
of negroes, "A perfectly stupid race can
never rise to a very high plane; the negro,
for instance, has been kept down as much by lack

of intellectual development as by
anything else."

Showing his full frontal double face
Washington says of Negroes, "Character, not
circumstances, makes the man."

"Call me Colonel," TR greets Washington, cordial.

Showing his full face duplicity Washington
says of others, "One man cannot hold another
man down in the ditch without remaining down
in the ditch with him."

The Tuskegee Wizard, no sluggard at Minstrel-
style face transplacing, doffs his homburg &, mindful
or not, miming Br'er Rabbit greeting Tar Baby,
replies, poker-faced, proper, precise as the place
settings, "Nice weather we're having, *Mister* President."
Washington plays 'em close to the vest with the
best of them.

TR, with his manor-born manner with the help,
ranch hands, aides, junior officers, non-coms, &
the enlisted, is on familiar terrain. &,
an aunt at baby Teddy's bedside renders Br'er
Rabbit yarns (along with overheated chestnuts
of the "queer goings on in the Negro quarters")
glommed on a pre-Proclamation plantation &
delineated by an uncle for print.

Joel Chandler Harris glimms & guts the same lode, &
mongered the boodle like bullion, profiting
&
making his name. The kipped tales have a common
West African origin with Pres Teddy's
trickster motto, "Speak softly & carry a big stick."

TR sees Booker T.'s feign, & trickster-a-
trickster, raises him a smile. "Glad you could come."

Bwana Tumbo (Master with a Big Stomach)
is TR's Swahili name on the dark side.

Booker doesn't blink or break a sweat. In high-stakes
showdowns his game's been stropped on a covey of
governors, former Chief Execs McKinley &
Harrison, & while taking tea with Victoria
the Queen of England. Then as now he masks his aims
behind shuck & humbug, parrying & mincing
until the other's hole card & intendments are
as plain as the no's on his face.

Pleasantries of protocol behind them, TR
kicks off the proceedings with entertaining re-
worked play-by-plays of his & Mr. Hearst's "splendid
little" expansionist 1898 15-week,
4-battle Spanish-American War.
                                        BT knows
it was more Theater of the Caribbean
than war; strutting Teddy, who'd prayed there'd be no peace
in the place before he arrived, left wife & son
bedridden behind (a pattern perhaps?) to ride
south, t'ward, he hoped, his moment of manifest
manliness.
                    His blood up, arrived in his bespoke
Brooks Brothers uniform & hand-lathed walking shoes;
cared for, along with his 2 horses, by his
"colored body-servant, former Indian fighter
Marshall," "the most faithful & loyal of men . . ." &
chronicled by his personal publicist, led
the Rough Riders, manned with buckaroos, veterans,
& assorted men of mark, shoulder to
segregated shoulder with Buffalo Soldiers—

Smoked Yankees, so called by Cubans, "boys" (wink & nod)
of the ("We Can. We Will.") (colored) 9th & ("Ready
& Forward") (colored) 10th Regular U.S.
Cavalry. They did . . . & did: "were black heroes,
every one of them," by eyewitness reports.

"We used to think the Negro didn't count for very much,
light fingered in the melon patch and chicken yards and such . . .
But we've got to reconstruct our view on color more or less
now we know about the 10th at Las Plasmas!"

Colored troops were brave, declares fight-hankering
Lt. Col. Roosevelt out of 1 side
of his mouth, while in his itchy, jingoistic
zeal (proof: he quits his Navy Department gig, turns
his back on the sickbeds of his women-folk, 1st
daughter & 2d wife, to jump down, spin around
& gallop off to war), where, in his impatience
takes unauthorized command, forces a trigger-
happy, self-ordered San Juan Hill advance (more mud-
slog than charge), bull-moosing through disciplined black ranks,
defaming them, out of the other side of the
same mouth "shirkers in their duties and would only
go as far as they went led by white officers."

& in ensuing battle's hurly burly is
the white New York 71st that is spooked, panics.
TR, nonplussed, insulting his own men,
threatening to shoot any who ran from his ill-
advised rush into enemy fire, storming
& steaming uphill like the choo choo that could,
stuttering, lurching, stumbling, once again, against
the haunting fear of the appearance of boyish
timidity, resulting in a higher
% of Rough Rider deaths, but more glory,
than any other volunteer regiment.

In his praising with faint damns account, Congressman
John F. Fitzgerald, JFK's granddaddy, says
"the black-skinned men who, with gleaming eyeballs and
shining teeth, rushed to the assistance of the Rough Riders."

"Occasionally they produce non-Commissioned
officers who can take the initiative," TR
concedes, "and accept responsibility
precisely like the best class of whites; but this can-
not be expected normally, nor is it fair
to expect it. . . ." Especially their, in his mind,
having to bear "the superstition and fear
of the darky, natural in those but one
generation removed from slavery and but
a few generations removed from the wildest
savagery."

Colored troopers had fewer courts-martial &
desertions than any other units in the U.S. army.

5 of the 10th are awarded Medals of Honor.
& in the actual heat of the actual
battle, the 9th, TR is loath to admit, was first
up the hill covered with as many darkies as
the best class of whites.

Without detail for detail, still & all it is,
Washington knows, a tragic-comedy of a
horseless cavalry, typhoid, jungle rot, yellow fever,
wounded & dead, but a boon & boost to press &
motion picture bottom lines. Washington knows it is,
in Mark Twain's words, "bandit's work under a flag," juiced
by bare-faced U.S. of A Imperialism,
as hell-bent on calling the tune for the unwilling
little coloreds of the Pacific Rim as the
colored practitioners of ragtime pounding out their

syncopated undermining of the Manifest
Destiny of mighty whiteness. "We have gone there
to conquer, not to redeem . . . ," Twain concludes, which has
"debauched America's honor and blackened her
face [wink & nod] before the world."

BT, polite, passes up a second helping
of chicken, knows the adventure ended with
Paris Treaty–approved Pacific territories,
10,000 miles tip to tip. Cuba, Guam, Puerto
Rico, the Philippines, talon-clutched in its mighty
grasp, beneath the spread of the Yanqui Eagle's
majestic wings.

Knows when the black rag-tag Johnnies, who'd "fought their way
into the hearts of the American people,"
returned, parading up the avenue out front,
"hailed as the most famous regiment of African
blood since Hannibal" with a band before & a
band behind, the men did cheer & the boys did shout
& the women did turn out; knows they stepped smartly,
& were saluted by pig iron manufacturer's
son President William McKinley.

Knows he, BT, is who & where he is because
he does not rattle the lion's cage, nor poke the bear.
"When your head is in the lion's mouth, use your hand
to pet him."

Many Rough Riders join Wild Bill's Wild West to-do,
for wages, "authentic" reenactments of their
taking of La Guasima, El Caney, San Juan,
& Kettle Hills.

Many hope blacks' heroic deeds at La Guasima,
El Caney, San Juan, & Kettle Hills will lead to
"a new era for the Negro race."

No. History repeats itself. It's still tough times
for negroes, including dwellers on Manhattan's
midtown rise, new named San Juan Hill, where tumble &
rough, bottle & brick brawls is oft' doing between
close-packed white & negro elements, ending
in Billy-club dispensed justice, &, more
memorably, from which will jump down, spin around
& around, the discrete & onliest, bearded,
ping-ponging, hat-wearing, stride-based pianist-
jazz composer of crippled-crab, between the cracks
ambulation tunes, Thelonious Sphere Monk,
1917–1982, who says,
"Everyone is influenced by everybody
but you bring it down home the way you feel it." Monk,
after his San Juan Hill descent, will change every-
thing.
De*dum*
de dum **dum** . . .

From down home to D.C., BT thinks, "varying in
color from dark-brown to black, brittle, combustible,
and very insoluble" like Kanawha coal,
in the mine from which I rose, is how they think of us.
I'm the lump with the carbon core that could be gold.
Carboniferous. *Carb,* coal, & *fero,* I bear.

COAL: step 1: Much as 3 to 4 million years ago
plant life, moss & trees & things buried beneath
sediment, minerals & rocks & sand & soil
& things settled to the bottom of rivers &
streams & things, & under pressure decay to form
compressed watery mass called peat.

Table bussed, cutlery accounted for, linen
down the chute, an interlude with Alice behind them,
alone in the room full of their contradictions,
they spend "the better part of the evening in talk

concerning the South." An average of 2 lynchings
per week Washington patiently, patently
quiescent points out, though on record says:
"The wisest among my race understand that the
agitation of questions of social
equality is the extremest folly."
                                        &
still it is a tough time for negroes. The
lynching statistics have held since 1892.

COAL: step 2: Compaction, serious vertical
pressure from accumulating mass, forces water
out of the peat, forms a soft, brown coal called lignite.

TR, animated, knowing he is who
& where he is by not expecting the blow but
delivering the blow, is brusque, doesn't blink or
break a sweat; a Bull Moose's marked deck trumps
a "Great Accommodator['s]" bluff every hand.

At evening's end, with all hands dealt & cards face up,
the Bull Moose breaks it down: "Sleeping dogs will be left
to lie." The status will be quo. "Thanks for dropping by."

COAL: step 3: Added pressure & time compress
the life out of lignite & form a soft substance
called bituminous coal.

The Wizard soft shoes to the door, "The honor is
mine." He's cut no deals & pockets no promises,
but with Douglass 6 years, 8 months a-moldering,
& only Du Bois as a stone in his passway,
there is more shortening in Booker's bread just for
having bellied to the Colonel's table.

He slouches on his hat & patient as coal, tips
out to the avenue. He feels like making tracks,
like laying his body down by home fires.

COAL: step 4: Combined pressure & the heat of
compaction transform the bituminous substance
to a hardness & luster almost pure carbon coal
called anthracite. Buried sunshine.

Moonless. A twinkle in the night-tide of the sky's
negritude. How much light gleamed & the measure?
As unknowable, in his mind, as how deep the coal's core.

Interlude
one

In Which There Are Considerations of Digging, Extracting, and Fear of Being Lowered into Hell

Mine.

Mining.

Miner.

Minor.

32°25' 53" N
85°42' 24" W
(32.431506,
-85.706781):
Tuskegee, Alabama

MINE: An excavation in the earth from which ore or minerals can be extracted. With shafts, & equipment.

MINING. **1.** The process of extracting ore or minerals from their source. **2.** The process of laying explosive mines.

Edison's biggest bust to date is his failed alchemy at turning low-grade iron ore into high-grade steel mill briquettes.

MINER: One whose work it is to extract ore or minerals from the earth & break it into "rag ore," or lumps, before sorting.

MINOR: Being under legal age.

Miners pick & blast photosynthesized bits & bobs: silt, residuum, chaff, swarf, skimmings, scoria,

scurf, off-scourings, odds & sods, e.g., "buried
sunshine," to be energy prehended from
carbon, & rag ore'd into trams.

Grainy cobweb of dank, rank, black-gray grit
cakes the tongues of engirdled, soot-shrouded "punters,"
bunch-backed boys & girls who grunt & drag rag ore drams &
scuttles to the main line to be hauled & hoisted
up & out, to heat & fuel America's
Forward March.

Young BT, at 9 years, dragged back each pre-morn
by the business of after-slavery, a pull
strong as natural or enacted law.

Young BT, lowered, each pre-morn, like a pail
down a well shaft, into the maw of the tar-dark
pitch-hole of the Virginia mountain.

                                        Always
the fear while being lowered into the Hell
of slag falls, dust, blasts, fires, & gaseous air, stale
as his daily bread: fear not of being choked, crushed,
burned, blown to scree, but swallowed, to wander without
end in the utter, ceaseless, brutish black beyond
black. Its pull so burly as to threaten no
escape for the un-wily, the weak.

"Associate yourself with people of good quality,
for it is better to be alone than in bad
company," Tuskegee's founder thinks.

Went to see TR, not on dais or caboose back,
but as lion in his lair; where he presides;
shuffles in slippers, lays his head. The better to
gauge the temper of his strength, the capacity
of his heart.

Which Treats of "The Great Negro Educator's" Sally along the Avenue; Frederick Douglass

NIGHT. PENNSYLVANIA AVENUE:
"America's main street." Lined with Lombardy poplars
planted by Thomas Jefferson; "a large and
direct avenue . . . proportioned to the greatness
which . . . the Capital of a powerful Empire
ought to manifest."
                         Poplars are popular
as the 1st choice of Southern lynchers.

A lone black figure in black enters the frame.
A streetcar clatter-rattles past. Clang-clang.

Up ahead, far as the darkness permits, BT
more senses than sees a black shape, shambling t'ward him
with a beggar's medium-slow gate.

Clang-Clang, Ding-Ding.

In D.C.'s West End 2-year-old baby

Edward Kennedy Ellington, Duke, is being
pampered pampered pampered.

& way down yonder in New Orleans 'mongst the myths
& dreamy scenes 73 days old Louis
Louie Daniel Satchmo Pops Armstrong will rise out
of Storyville, & while pushing piston valves &
blowing through molded brass, change everything.

In Chicago, 50 days hence, Walt Disney will
see his first flickering light. He too will be famous.

Clang-Clang-Ding-Ding.

The Pennsylvania Avenue streetcar, that
any colored or white can, for a nickel, 6
tickets for a quarter, ride, no questions asked, heads,
Ding, Ding, on its electrified 3d rail toward
Anacostia out of the frame & across
the bridge.
            Sojourner Truth, an Underground Railroad
conductor, manhandled (isn't she a woman?) by
a D.C. streetcar conductor who, back when the fare
is a penny, does not want to let her ride. She
sues. Truth, to the benefit of coloreds, wins.

No. As it nears its not dark-town off-stride strut, but
more shamble than amble, as if approaching
in an Edison film with every other frame
blank or blackened, but, still as if any second
might break into a herky-jerky jubaed caper
& twirl.

Ouuua Ooga!, clip-clopping, cl—ackety clackclack.

Still it is a tough time for negroes. *Ouuua Ooga!*

Couples hunch into each other, hushed. Hurry by.

The bridge, in 1940, will be named for John
Phillip Sousa, 2, 3, 4.

An automobile heads south; another, *Ouuua ooga!*

& from off taptapping from the figure with dog
& hickory cane approaching interval by
interval through yellow-gray parentheses
of gaslight, like a buoy on a sea of black,
bobbing closer & closer, taking on detail
at each sighting & stick's clearer taptapping.

The Capitol lies, slightly off geographic
center of the city, at the straight line (over
the Circles as the crow flies) of the avenue's
far end. Where, until 3 score & 9 years ago
slaves, within a shackle's rattle, were sold. 2,3,4.

Figure, like darkness within darkness, closer now.
Sees him, head to foot, a pool away. Hickory stick
& yellow-gray cur, paw-nails click-clicking with each
guarding step, & the cane's tip tap-tapping.
                                        Like some
haint, BT thinks; plantation phantasm, haunting.
Thinks: Like those beyond Tuskegee's creed & reach. Closer.
Emerges into the same sphere of light. Clearer
for that moment in gas-glow's illuming; though close
enough to touch with a half-raised hand, seen as if
through a skein of cobwebs or fly ash.
                                        Clothed in deep-
worn, scarecrow threadbare.
                                Click-clicking, tap-tapping, &
muttering—the best forgotten worst of the modes
& means of slavery expression: yawning thick-

tongued intonation, rough, glottal, guttural as
ass brays, dark, dirty-toned phrases mangled as briars;
sing-song; dense-drenched in mine-sweat as the wrenched
haulers of a shift's-worth of coal. Hears him. Drawling-
no-purpose-lay-about-mush-mouth, echoing clock-
work click-clicking & drearisome, timeless tap-tapping
of man & cur's measured stride.
                                           2-3-4 . . . as their
paths cross.

Horse & rider: *clip clop* smartly by.

Blues they call it. Anti-melodic mouthings, dark-
choked as post-flood Mississippi flotsam. Low lyrics
looking for trouble, or licking their lips over
reckless love. Its bile-bitterness & tap-tapping
stops BT up short.
                          Freezes him.

Our music should have naught to do with common
throaty groans. No idler's squalls, caterwauls; should be
heartening uplift; cure for outrages' woes. Not
that shift's-end coal-black miner's-back-in-Malden mood.
Be—Pleasant. Pleasing. Like my dear mama, Jane,
rest her sweet soul, humming & stirring my porridge
in that dented, little blackened pot. Yes. Pick &
plait them, like old plantation songs, from the sacred
side; though music of bondage, they were work-
together ditties, with dignity, that tempered
task's distaste. "Swanee River," "Old Kentucky Home,"
& such. No tunes birthed in covetous sloth, or fueled
by ambition beyond authorities' intentions.

Like waking from a dream, his heart pounding—BT
turns. The figure, like a sigh, is not there. Is gone.

Cl—ackety Clackclack.

BT wonders about the muttered cadenced words
as he still hears beneath his heel's measured tread,
the off-rhythmic counter chorus of echoing
mine shaft water's icy leaking
                              plip
                              plop
                              plip
                              plopping
down the heart of his spine as he walks with the same
determination as 28 years ago—

Away from the dreaded black-dark of Malden Mine,
at Kanawha, West Virginia. Walks & begs.
Blisters size of coal lumps; legs shaft-timber heavy;
stomach empty as a rust-sieved pail. Walks
the 500 miles across state's line to Hampton
Normal & Agricultural Institute,
                              on a rumor & a hope.

TE's film troops shoot-it-if-it-moves events
of spectacle, note, & *common* interest: populist
flicker & flutter pleasing to every-day
Americanist consumers, e.g., baboons
bicycling, flexing musclemen in tights, bustled
women, McKinley's funeral, the 1901
Pan-American Exposition, donkey acts,
farmers, firemen, a bag-punching dog, boxing
sisters, an ecdysiast on a trapeze, leap-
frogging Esquimaux, faux Indians, smoke, boom &
motion of Spanish-American & Boer War
skirmishes reenacted in New Jersey: a grab-
bag sampling of scenes screened between-acts during
evenings of vaudeville, a role filled by minstrel skits
at the form's formation.

But, due to their dereliction, through ignorance,
intent, or indifference, no moving image
of the lone figure, America's 1st & most
powered negro, exiting the newly named White
House, after supping with the Bull Moose, was fit to film.

Just as there's no footage of Malden Mine's shift's end,
à la *Sortie des Usines Lumière a Lyon*
(*Workers Leaving the Lumière Factory*) by
Auguste & Louis, the groundbreaking French brothers
Lumière; the coal at its underground core grime-ground
into every miner & minor emerging,
burnt-corked-black as minstrels, eyes bucked in the light
at the end of the tunnel. They doff their caps, puff
out their stunted candles, & in funereal
lock-step, slow as a plow mule at sunset, or
cortege stallion hauling a president's coffin,
drag their scraggy shadows along home, 2, 3, 4.

Ouuua ooga!

"Movies," Auguste Lumière said, "was an invention
without a future." The Frenchman didn't continue
the quote to include the American Negro,
also an invention. Lumière meant, *sans* story,
a tale told, yarn spun, fiction or fact, the fledging
form (as well as the unmentioned Negro) was
simply what it already was, amusement, &
would grow to be nothing more.

Cl—ackety Clackclack.

So, no, there is no camera's eyewitness as BT
walks off his exhaustion, as there is no footage
of Frederick Douglass, rest his weary soul, who in
late life lives on Cedar Hill. Anacostia,

across the Potomac. In eyesight of the Capitol.
2-story house. Brick symbol of his rise; slave to
spokesman of his Negro people.

No 1890s early morning, landing level
shot: Douglass's gray bramble of hair rising as he,
hand on rail, scales the steps to a full-span view.
In floor-length housecoat. A gift, mauve, purple piping
& plaited rope sash.

"The black Daniel Webster," stands at an attic porthole.
Over-his-shoulder perspective, through the round window,
his home's eyeball, we see, across the river, like
a spiked Klan helmet, the distant white dome,
legislative seat of the United States of
America, housing Congress, whose laws he has
challenged for ½ a century.

The site whose very foundation was quarried, shaped,
& hauled & set in place by my brothers, enslaved
& free, he thinks. Whose walls, floors, & ceilings were hewed
& sawed & planed, hammered, sanded, plastered, & caulked
by those for whom it is a symbol, then as now,
of the city's & Democracy's heart of
hypocrisy.

Reverse perspective through window's exterior.
Moving closer as Douglass, former Baltimore
slave, sips from his cup of steaming chicory.
Continuing closer. His face fills the screen.
Closer, tighter. His eye fills the screen. Tighter. Till
camera seems to enter his eye. Screen, if such film
existed, would go to BLACK. Soot, boot, crow, pitch, lamp,
ink, cat, fetid, sinful, plague, death, mourning, black BLACK.

No stock of Eastman Kodak celluloid

cranks steady as Sousa music through a sniper-
still camera, letting light shaft through the shutter's
jackrabbit-fast winking & blinking winking &
blinking . . .

No record for scholars to read, frame by grainy
blown-up, stop-motioned frame, of the criss-crossing black
forms with diverse gaits, fluxing to a spectrum
of Seurat-like spackled & sparkling coal dust static;
indecipherable black-white-noise for the eye.

Washington, left hand in his overcoat pocket,
satchel in his right, through the heart of the district,
toward the Central Market, that sold groceries,
& dry goods &, until 40 years ago, black men,
women, & children in good order & fit for
immediate service.

The looming dome like a ½ moon of ice.
Douglass 6 years, 9 months dead, *May he rest in peace.*
6 years 1 month from BT's own Atlanta
Exposition Address when whites & blacks, awed,
inaugurate & anoint Principal Washington,
simple schoolteacher, to the position of New
Leader of the Negroes.

A spokesman protests, BT thinks, barks, heel-nips,
evaluates. A leader . . . *Elevates* . . .

& like a sigh, 2, 3, 4, the passing man's speech-
less words escape BT's hearing. He fleeting feels,
but not.

Ding-Ding.
Ouuua ooga!
Cl—ackety Clackclack.

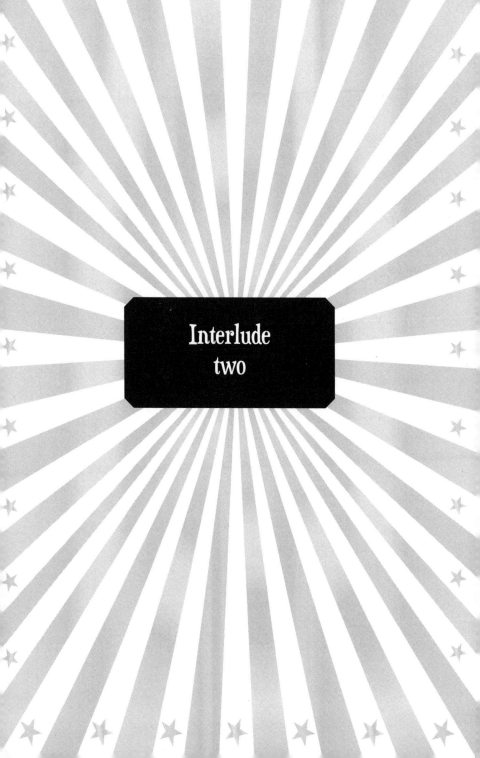

Interlude
two

A Delineation in Alice's Wonderland; & an Infrequent, Imagined Nightmare

Alice Roosevelt, 17, will, if allowed,
crawl, like a still clawed cat, onto her daddy's lap.
Motherless child, anxious for a good time to show
off her knowledge, folds her napkin.

Alice Roosevelt (1884–19-
80), TR's eldest.

What are they doing at Tuskegee, Alice wonders?
Are they like your children? What songs do they sing &
do you let them dance? Questions with 2 faces, one,
of wise wonder, for him, the other, its tongue stuck out,
for her daddy.
                    2 days old when her mother died.

Her father lit out for the territory, was
a ghost during her leg-brace-bound early years, grieved
on some lone prair-re, *recasting himself to*
no longer need nestling of mother, wife, or child,
but to be brethren with the picturesque, the bold,
the fearless breed of his race who forged forward, cut
trails, led the white advance.
                    Her father, with power
to wage wars & bust trusts, beams enthralled. She is a
problem solvable by strict restraint & proper
supervision, but daddy will skin no switch, give
her no taste of domestic policy with his
lickin' stick. Does not raise his voice, counsel restraint,
or shorten the bridle to rein her in, who
fancies herself "allergic to discipline."

Announces she, a home-schooled, 10 o'clock scholar,
read his book. No. Yes. "... born a slave on a plantation
in Franklin County, Virginia ..." The Story of
My Life and Work, *by Booker T. Washington, "with*
over Half a Hundred Full-Page Photos and Half-
tone Engravings and Drawings" by Frank Beard, published
1900. Yes.

Tells her he is working on a revision, Up
from Slavery. *He must send her a copy.*
Promises. But that is not the end of it. To
prove she has done her homework, unsolicited,
unrestrained, reenacts his story. Delineates,
through recitation, mime, dance, & tableaux, his life
quoting "just another little nigger"*; white-*
washing race matters, spotlights fortitude (self-will):
his long walk to Tuskegee; book learning; brick-
making, building: McKinley's visit; on she goes,
center of attention, Alice Blue, performing,
BT knows, to lighten her (wispy) burden
of boredom & blahs. In need-feed self-reinvention,
watching, furtive as a thief, for her father's dis-
proving approval, as she, strutting back & forth,
mimes speeches given: his first at Hampton; & most
recent—casting down his bucket in Atlanta;
choreographed separate fingers of a hand;
as she, before her father's eyes, & in her mind,
shifts from who she is, through who she isn't, toward
who she wishes to be, him—at 17, &
in a dress, huntress/discoverer of a well-
spring of Brahmin to bohemian unruliness
(of the dewy sort to stir discomfort in her
daddy, dowagers, & other crème).

Stalking through, as far as she knows, vestal terrain,
but in BT's view is merely miner/punter—

*picking & spading in the darkness of her
ignorance & intent from the lode of his life;
hauling drams of re-cast meaning to fuel the dustup
in a teacup of her (flimsy) Up from Privilege
insubordination.*

BT pictures a pre-show minstrel with smudge pot,
facing a mirror, smoothing blacked palms about
a darkening countenance.

*The Bull Moose, in that light, reduced to the twin glint
ovals of his pince-nez lens, laughing, high pitched
as a sherry-tipsy matron, brashly satisfied.*

BT thinks, *The things you have to do to do
the things you have to do.*

*Watches, shamming interest in her ineptitude.
Watches, as if he is addled by its shimmer
& sold on the face value of her implied
conspiratorial kinship.*
          *He is not
amused by her hackneyed, Minstrel-tradition
portrayal, the naïveté of her presumptions,
or the audacity of her bamboozling mis-
calculations about his life & work. Her im-
perfect understanding evidences no true
interest in his character, save to blacken it.
& though its face is softer tinged than true minstrelsies'
visual raunch, its intent is seditious still.*

*Being the President's daughter & not some grime-
necked exile with olde worlde broagh, patois, or pidgin
tied to his tongue, does not cast it new & improved,
but, yet another way they've found to steal his scuttle
for to haul their ashes in, haul their ashes in.*

Oh, to do the things you have to do.

Alice will continue her minstrel ways. Will trumpet
"Fill what's empty. Empty what's full. Scratch where it itches."
She will be a self-defined hedonist; become
a party favor Talk of the Town novelty
act, a sensation: bet on the ponies, wear a
boa for a boa, blow smoke from the White House
rooftop, dance the Turkey Trot like a "shinny
leopard cat," wolf down pork chops, & take pot shots from
whistle stops at telegraph poles, & plutocrat
politicos.
             &, for the no-no of taking
illicit liberties with purloined source
materials, will invoke the Loas, & will
get no satisfaction. She'll be Alice Blue for true.
Will marry a playboy, her father's junior by
only 11 years. She will bear an outside child.
The fruit of her loins will discover her own dark
side; will, at 31, kill herself.

Hum hm h*mummm*

BT will not report the dream of Alice's
recital to Margaret or the boys; not mention
it to donors, colleagues, students, nor note it in
journal or oration. But, like the plip
                              plop, will
not forget.

Still it is a tough time for negroes.

2-3
Hum hm huum*mummm*

How long?

4

Wherein Are Related Matters Trifling & Historic, Lame-Brained & Etymological, Relating to Jim Crow & His Formidable Rise

"We will now discuss in a little more detail
the Struggle for Existence."—Charles Darwin.

Midst the furor following Washington's visit
it is said, "the White House is so saturated
with the odor of the nigger that the rats
have taken refuge in the stable."

&, "No Southern woman with proper self-respect
would now accept an invitation to the White House."

"Doesn't make any difference who we are or
what we are," quoting the quotable Twain, "there's
always somebody to look down on." & "Ignorance,"
saith Darwin, "more frequently begets confidence
than does knowledge . . ."

BT with his mind on traveling, his mind on home,
down the track he rides with each wheel go-round of the
locomotive's lurch & lunge rolling him back down
to de cotton & de cor'n where the mood of Pitchfork
Ben Tillman is still on the move in Alabam'.

"If the misery of the poor be caused not by
the laws of nature, but by our institutions,
great is our sin." —Charles Darwin.

"Names, once they are in common use, quickly become
mere sounds, their etymology being buried,
like so many the earth's marvels, beneath the dust
of habit." —Salman Rùshdie, novelist, b.
1947.

Etymology of the Jim in Jim Crow: Jim,
takes flight as Ya'akov, or, Ya'agob, meaning
"heel catcher," "supplanter," "leg puller," tripper upper,
displacer by stratagem, superseder,
overthrower, underminer, then morphs to
Jacob, the Genesis twin, holding brother
Esau's heel at birth, trying to hold him back.
Later Jacob, desperate for undeserved blessings
& privileges, offers to swap a bowl of stew
for his starving brother's birthright (to be
recognized as 1st born).
In Espanola Jim is Iago, spiteful,
amoral, malevolent, Shakespearean trickster.
Irony abounds.

& Crow:
Noun. From Old English *crāwe*. Related to Old Norse
kráka, Old High German *kraia*, Dutch *kraai*.
      craw [kraw]. Contemptible big carnivorous black bird.
      crow

Verb

1. past crowed or crew (of a cock); to utter a
shrill squawking sound. 2. to boast
about one's superiority — Idiom
stick in one's craw, to cause considerable or
abiding resentment; rankle: I'm an un-
lawful law, I really stick in their craw.

Crow: a derogatory term for a black man.

During TR's tenure Jim Crow rises, burrows,
spreads; higher, deeper, wider. Backed by the gilded
& most progressive anthropological,
biological, theological, psycho-
logical, sociological, political,
& medical minds of the times, colored voting
numbers dive, poll taxes rise, throat-cutting clauses
are grandfathered in: the doors to white colleges,
= housing, & public facilities slam.
The floodgates of disparity burst wide open.

An inundation of Jim Crow. New South (re)new(ed)
segregations & restrictions. Here a law, there
a law, everywhere an illicit law on what
they can & can't, & with whom, where, & how; an
afflux, conflux, reflux, surfeit, glut, piss down
to hem them in under penalty of Law &
punishment at every jump down spin around.

Hear,
e.g., the brassy oompa oompa oompa oom-
pa of a New Orleans marching band — (their origins
in the 1830s). See the new Jim Crow laws,
& in their wake, second-lining right along,
leveling New Orleans' ethnic playing field
by knocking up-town, European-favoring,

music-reading Creoles (segregated (or, as
they would have it, separated) by the tone
of their skin, accent, ancestry, & airs) down
into the (small s) society of Story-
ville, with its dark-skinned, Africa-inclined,
ear players—& their lowly allegiances to
field hollerers & Congo Square dancers, adding
to the rolls of those who have, & play the blues.
This enforced social & cultural potpourri
stirs, simmers, & serves up a new stew: a 2-step,
slow drag gumbo, crude & blue, but one both their folks
can sure dance to.

See,
e.g.,
Reckoning with redneck 'rithmetic Pitch-
fork Ben posits, "the action of . . . Roosevelt in
entertaining the nigger will necessitate
our killing a thousand niggers in the South before
they will learn their place again." Follow the numbers.

Another good ol' fire-eating Southern boy
confessed, ". . . Booker Washington is a smart
'nigger' and way above the average, but at the
same time he is a 'nigger' just the same."

From Alabama's constitutional
convention, 21 May–September 3,
1901, convenes in the hall of the House
of Representatives, Montgomery. John B. Knox,
Esq., President, Pat McGauly, Esq.,
Official Stenographer, ". . . the negro is
the prominent factor in the issue." Its sole
mission is to restore the "rest and peace and
happiness" of the pre-XV Amendment times,
for "if we would have white supremacy, we must

establish it by law—not by force or fraud." (wink
& nod). But the disfranchising of blacks, they must
have, without question or delay.
Reconstruction, such as it is, & has been,
is out, deconstruction in. Do Derria Dah.
When BT's train rolls into Alabama he
holds his tongue. On the 57th day,
the convention delegates, satisfied, nod their heads
& slowly walk away.

"I love fool's experiments."—Charles Darwin.

"If I had a world of my own, everything would
be nonsense," Lewis Carroll, a.k.a. Charles Lutwidge
Dodgson (1832–98), English
author, Anglican deacon, logician, &
mathematician, has Alice, in his *Alice's
Adventures in Wonderland*, say, "Nothing would be
what it is," she continues, "because everything
would be what it isn't. And contrary wise, what
is, it wouldn't be. And what it wouldn't be, it
would. You see?"

Unanimous word goes out from the convention
which codifies Jim Crow & disenfranchises
women in the bargain: "I am a white man. I am
proud of my race, proud of my blood, proud of my
ancestors, proud of my lineage, proud of my country,
proud of my State, and proud of the fact that I live . . .
under a government that is willing to do
justice to all people of all races. I want
to call attention to the fact that the white people
of this State own all of the lands. . . . They own all
the money, they own all the houses, they do all
the business, they own all the banks, they sell all
the goods, they practice all the law, they hold all the offices,

from the Governor down to bailiff. They have control
of the militia, they have got all the guns,
they have got all the telegraphs and railroads and telephones
and furnaces and factories and foundries.
They have got the education, they have got a thousand
years' advantage of the negro race in civilization."

(A raised hand all the way in the back goes un-
recognized. His question, "So then what's the problem?"
goes unasked.)

"I for one am proud that I belong to the white race,
I am proud to stand here today, and state in my place,
that I believe that God Almighty made the white
man superior in the beginning, and with
all of the advantages that we have over
the negro, I am not afraid of the negro.

"If we disfranchise the great body of Negroes,"
an Alabama conventioneer concludes,
"let us do so openly and above board and
let there be an end of all sorts of jugglery."
(Wink & nod.)

Jim Crow's Song,
with faint nod to minstrelsy's Topsy.

Way down south in de cotton and de corn,
I just growed, I never was born;
My old nigra's used to say,
Dat I warn't no good, only gets in de way.

I used to dance, I used to sing,
From darkies I did thieve,
Sho did do that thing.
& since you ask,

Yes, I did revise;
I've slipped the mask before your eyes,
& all that implies.
Shho did do that thing.
Changed my game
But my aim remains the same.
No more tricks up the sleeve,
Attempt to deceive, I'm in tune
With the current trend.
I've deep-sixed delineation
In favor of legislation
That makes blacks blue without end.

Interlude
three

In Which Is Related an Imagined Concert by Imagined Professor Lyons at Tuskegee

Tuskegee, "Warrior" in the Muskhogean
(Muskogee) dialect of the Creek language.

Meanwhile, on the Normal School for Colored Teachers
at Tuskegee campus, where Thrift & Patience &
the Godliness of Dirt-Scratching & By-Scraping
head the curriculum. There are queer goings-on.

Professor Lyons, mathematics instructor from
Columbus O., short on patience with whites after
barred by a bitter suite of Jim Crow orchestrated
backs turned & doors slammed in the face
of foolhardy aspiration—tutoring t'ward
a classical music career; hardened, settles
for the democracy of absolute value,
axis of symmetry, common factors, parallels,
& numerical logic.

On occasional evenings, when frustration
at conditions Hell, west, & crooked rise in him
like weatherglass mercury, he steals in
where, at room's rear a donated piano rests,
between little Old Glorys on sticks, & black-framed
Republican presidents glowering from their place
above the slate boards where that day's lessons
in saleable skills & acceptance of social
realities were chalked in neat cursive script.

Lyons plays.

Passersby, their Bible & broom duties done, hear,

ease in, hushed, watch the random recital. Someone
runs to tell others. *Hurry!* They, collars loosened,
jackets & aprons off, join to hear him plaiting
& yoking, stacking & stringing out quadrilles &
arias & marches & waltzes, with the new
syncopated cadences of blue-black music's
raddled, multipart harmonic displacements on
colored spirituals, & good ol'-time gospel
shouts; new rollicking, black style musical oil &
water, or cornbread & buttermilk conversations
Principal Washington would deem indecorous.

It is, it is—well, is like a monkey on a
buzzard's back; along for the ride but jumping or
bumping to its own cut-loose rhythm, as its host
flap-flaps, 1,2 steadily along, 3, 4,
with each pieced & patched note shape-shifting shift-shaping
to its own needs, & it's all . . . while the cat's away . . .
they can humanly do to keep from singing &
dancing 'round the potbellied stove.
                                        Is, some wonder,
the of-the-minute concoction they're hearing
design? coincidence? serendipity? luck?
accident? or score settling?
                          For, though he never
says, nor never dare they ask, they discern, without decoding
note for note, it is music in condemnation
of that nasty black bird, who just growed, never was born;
turning from jokesman to spokesman, entertainer
to restrainer, who tangles the traces to the
plow of their life; puts chiggers in the grits of their
liberty; clogs the flue & backs smoke up in the
house of their security; puts soot in the soup
of their pursuit of happiness; boll weevils
in the patch of their equal protection; holes
in the roof of their peaceful assembly &

association; blood on the moon of their pre-
sumed innocence; rust in the water of the well
of their opinion & expression; & sics Hell's
hounds on their defense against arbitrary
arrest & detention.

      & when Lyons is through
the sum of his notes & rhythms & suspected
reasons ringing, pedal-pointed in their chests &
crania, they slip away with non-applauded
awe, & he sits a spell, like an engine coming
to rest after a long uphill haul.

Which Treats of the Last Stop of the Montgomery & West Point Railroad before BT's Return to Tuskegee, & Philosophical/ Political Musings on Music & Time Travel

After hours & miles over the cyclic
rolling-rattling rush, dozing, like at the Oaks, rain
against the pane, Margaret at her duties, sons
at their books, house-boy in the parlor, scuttling ashes,
then shaken awake by chords like steel squeaks & off-
rhythm tick-clicking-clacking over loose couplings
from that defiant Professor Lyons's off-
hours practice, clattering across paved or tarred
crossways.
        *Next stop Tuskeg*ee!

On schedule, the short dog's engine hisses, huffs,
down-chugs like a fat man sitting on a flour sack.

Gray billows roll back, rise to his window at the
rear, wander the tracks, cinders, & weeds at depot's

rump-end like a snuffling hound, then disappear
with listless indifference in blazing red dusk.

Suffocating as the mine. Washington lowers
the window, hat a fan against soot, stench, stifle.
Plop plip. Whites lade freight on board. In the fenced siding
at the yard's rear, 2 colored boys, bent like coolies,
muscle hundred-pound coal sacks from the railcar flatbed
to a one-horse dray.

Craves home: The Oaks. Margaret. The boys. A bath. His bed.
These 2, types his institute tutors in letters;
hygiene; industry; knife & fork mechanics; &
when, & when not—but impossible to tell, their
features & clothes rendered to sparkling-gray-black pall
by the grimy sacks they haul.
                                    One sings, in a voice
like speaking, if it *is* singing, if they *are* words;
are *more* like country-coarse sound-phrases for feelings.
The other whistles, though there is, to BT's ear,
no discernable tune. Just scrape-whine whistling, like
the sharp screech of tram wheel against rail—or keening
shrill of scooped shovel blade, sparking against bedrock.

BT recalls, with a shudder, a bird—once—
that he first feared was a bat—that has somehow
gotten down the shaft into the mine's deep. Screeches,
flutters blindly. Beats its wings, its twittering,
raging fear ricocheting off Malden's carbon-
walled black innards. BT often has snapped
remembrances of by-gone instances. Flashing
clicks, that linger as goose bumps, or sweat along his
nape & hairline. Plip plop.
                                    The hobbled horse snorts
in its feedbag. Chaws.
                                    Are the "singing," & "whistling,"

accompaniment for each other? Is it for the
2 of them alone? Or for any who hears? Or
are they random sounds, like a clearing of the throat,
or grunts or wheezes under the weight of the work?
It is hard to tell at his remove, as they criss-
cross, shuttling like lignite lumps on a loom, moving
a mountain of heat & fuel a sack at a time.

The bird trapped down the shaft, as BT recalls with
razor clarity—was a House Wren, whose song, when
at peace, he is put in mind of by the whistler's
trill: a lively prattle, rising then dropping
to fast-ending flurry—then repeat, repeat, repeat.
The singer's wavering tones drawn-out as dusk's murk
'long the horizon, far as the eye can see ("O
cant you see it"). & the whistler, a hiccupy-
halt in his shuffle, lugs, train to dray, back & forth,
forth & back, sings, in a slow-slurred ooze, like blood
from a coal-shard gouge, or gash on rusty barbed wire.

Remembers, without reason, the *tink* of ladle
& gilt-handled porcelain tureen on the side-
board, & the server of the White House soup. Dark,
in coat white as crisp snow. Their eyes never met, but
felt the pride & deep devotion to the task
humming from him like words through wire, or down-home
    hymns.

Hmmmmmmmmmm.

But at that moment BT minds not the meeting
behind him, flock business ahead, nor, in his view,
the lack of ample respect for open-air labor's
glories displayed by the mindless black boys' noise,
whose words at that distance he cannot hear, but knows
are without connection to refined music, or

matters of consequence to other than them. It
certainly isn't bound to anything beyond
the moment. Certainly it, if there is an *it*,
will last no longer than Quitting Time's call, their shift's
end, & they go on, off to whatever chore or
frisk occupies their idle time till morning come.
Surely their clamor is no deeper than the strange,
untrained mode of their locution, & is not fit,
or suitably refined, for the needed uplift
of the Negro mass in the time of their great need.

He half hopes they're not Tuskegee alumni, not
forms of vocational labor into which he'd
poured measures of morals & gratitude, & mixed
& made them surrogates of himself, for if he
had they had failed him—were not coinage minted in
Tuskegee's mold.
        So, longing solely for home, Margaret,
the boys, a bath, his bed, BT dismisses them.

Engineer & station master, pocket watch in hand,
crack wise. The boxcar door slides, slams like a shot.
Boo-oard!

Next stop, Tuskegee. Toot Toot! Home. Margaret. The
boys. A bath. His bed. Bone-weary. Plip-plop. Rock-sway.
Drift. Thinks. Chehaw to Tuskegee. 6 miles of
4' 8"-gauge steel track, laid by slave labor
before the War. Thinks:

In trying to make it from 1 point (or state of
the Union, or mind), say, to some other, say—say
—slavery to freedom, just to say—well Jim Crow
Ummhumm & Zeno, within the boundaries of their
logic, will tell you that, naturally, before
you get *all* the way, at some point, smooth or easy,

you'll be ½ your way, to the mid-point, say, just
to say, at which point you'll *still,* before you get *all*
the way, have ½ the way to go to get to where
you set out to get to be to where you set out
to be, but *before* you do get *all* the way, you'll
still, smooth or easy, get to a point where you'll *still*
have ½ way to go before you get *all* the way,
to *that* mid-point, say, just to say, at which point you'll
still, before you get all the way, have ½ the way
to go to get to where you set out to get to
to be to where you set out to be, but before you
do get *all* that way, you'll *still,* smooth or easy,
only get to a point where you'll *still* have ½ way
to go before you get *all* the way to that next
½ way, & so on & &c,
& &c, & so on, & so on, just
to say, no matter how close you get, you've still have
to go that last ½ way. Which, will, for the ex-slave
trying to rise to freedom, just to say, be for-
ever, or never, if Jim Crow (*Ummhumm*) & Zeno,
within the boundaries of their time-stopping logic,
have their way.

BT think-dozes:
In a race, to clock it another way, once Whites
get a jump, their lesson is, trying to catch up
is futile, foolish, failure bound, & the black laggard
is, & will remain, sluggard, slacker, tail dragger,
loser, always arriving late; where whites were
after they've been there & gone, so always &
forever doomed never to draw level. This,
the logic of the supremacist, slants, shapes, bends
by the weight of their need to be, by any
other name or means, necessary, Most, Utter,
Acme, All Meaning, First, The Last Word, Prime Mover,
Roost Ruler, Reins Holder, Absolute Perfection

(& are not scared of negro. No No.), is, in their
smug, imagined reality, shiny & puffed
as soap bubbles.

Rock sway, rock sway plip plop plip plop drip dripping down
the shaft of his spine.

Interlude
four

In Which There Is a Discourse on White, Purity, & Blood Lust

white (hwahyt, wayht)
The American Heritage® Dictionary
of the English Language, Fourth Edition ©
2000 by Houghton Mifflin Company. Up-
dated in 2003. Published by Houghton
Mifflin Company All rights reserved.
"*n.*
1. The achromatic color of maximum
lightness; the color of objects that reflect nearly
all light of all visible wavelengths; the complement
or antagonist of black. . . . Although typically
a response to maximum stimulation of
the retina, the perception of white appears
always to depend on contrast. **2.** . . . **e.** A white
breed, species, or variety of animal.
f. also **White** A member of a racial group
of people having light skin coloration,
especially one of European origin. . . .
4. *Games* **a.** The white- or light-colored pieces, as
in chess. **b.** The player using these pieces. . . .**7.**
A politically ultraconservative
or reactionary person. *adj.* **whit·er,**
whit·est 1. Being of the color white; devoid
of hue, as new snow. **2.** Approaching the color white,
as: **a.** Weakly colored; almost colorless; pale. . . .
c. Bloodless; blanched. . . . **4.** voting patterns within
the white population. **5.** Not written or
printed on; blank. **6.** Unsullied; pure."

Know in the whiteness of their bones, their gristle &
gut, know, in the face of the new, the Ol' South has

lost face, & a step or 2; isn't what it used
to be, back when it was when it could still pretend
to be what it pretended it was: White. Pure. Pure
as new snow.

"**pu·ri·ty** (pyoor-i-tee)
n.
1. The quality or condition of being pure.
2. A quantitative assessment of homo-
geneity or uniformity. 3.
Freedom from sin or guilt; innocence; chastity:
*"Teach your children . . . the belief in purity
of body, mind and soul"—Emmeline Pankhurst.* 4.
The absence in speech or writing of slang or other
elements deemed inappropriate to good style.
5. The degree to which a color is free
from being mixed with other colors.
Purity. Purity. Purity.
purity—the state of being unsullied by
sin or moral wrong; lacking a knowledge of evil
sinlessness,
whiteness,
innocence,
pureness
condition, status—a state at a particular
time; "a condition (or state) of disrepair,"
. . . cleanness—without moral defects—a
woman's virtue or chastity, pureness, honor,
sexual morality, chastity, virtue—
morality with respect to sexual relations."

Above & following from: *The American
Heritage® Dictionary of the English Language,
Fourth Edition,* copyright ©2000 by
Houghton Mifflin Company. Updated in
2003. Published by Houghton Mifflin Company.
All rights reserved.

Seeing as how a new balance needs to be
struck, a new un-balanced (in their favor) force
is necessary to right the out-of-kilter ship
of the state of current affairs, in the name
of the mechanism of social control, re-
establish homogeneity &
uniformity . . . & freedom from being mixed
with other colors.

Can't taint if they aint.

"**taint** (teynt)
v. **taint·ed, taint·ing, taints**
v.tr.
1. To affect with or as if with a disease.
2. To affect with decay or putrefaction;
spoil. . . . 3. To corrupt morally. 4. To affect
with a tinge of something reprehensible.
v.intr.
To become affected with decay or
putrefaction; spoil.
n.
1. A moral defect considered as a stain
or spot. . . . 2. An infecting touch, influence, or
tinge."

On the subjects of white & purity, President
Theodore Roosevelt says: "it is obvious
that if in the future racial qualities are
to be improved, the improving must be wrought
mainly by favoring the fecundity
of the worthy types [CODE WORD! CODE WORD!]. . . . At present,
we do just the reverse. There is no check to the
fecundity of those who are subnormal. . . ."

A question from the balcony, Doctor. *Caint taint*
if they aint *what?*
Aint!, caint taint,
where we live, eat, sleep, ride, walk, work, shop, worship, learn,
play, legislate. Just aint. But are in their place:
barefoot, hamstrung, & country.

& the answer is—?
Simple, to re-impose their lost civility,
decorum & manner.
& — ?
There must be a legitimized mandated
abomination, a sorcerer's concoction
of Diseased, Decayed, Putrefied, Spoiled, Corrupt, Stained
motions & potions in their most unbalanced, least
civil means imaginable: Lunatic, Sadistic,
Paranoid, Psychotic piss down; meant to halt
the heavenly orbs in their arc, block the hands &
sands of the clock; stop time, devise a reversal
of forward motion—a rewind to the lie
of the purity of absolute position
& an un-tainted past we cling to like a toddler
to its blanket, or tit.

But Einstein puts forward how—how—well—how *relative*
it all is; countermanding Supreme Court & old-
school stances of absolute position. Says it
is illusion, a false show, a pay-to-see
curiosity, a Barnumesque tadpole
on a lily pad shouldering a whale. Is
Caucasoid confusion, unsupportable by
psychology, science, or reason.

But what better psychic-cleansing, logic-defying
device is there than the hunt; when man is most un-

restrained; free to follow the natural callings
& rhythms of his heart & blood; when he is most man.

See,

> *Hold it—*
> *shutter click-snap!*

See

naturalist, conservationist Bwana
Tumbo, Teddy Roosevelt (Master with a Big
Stomach), in untamed topography, utterly
unknown to outsiders, hand on head of his hanging
prey, other 'round the barrel of his thunderstick.
Left eye asquint under the capitol dome
of his big white hunter's hat. At his side a dusky
native son, his sartorial twin, who's led the way
& done the work.

Roosevelt Game List (partial):
Water buffalo, elephant, eland, leopard,
lion, hyena, rhino, warthog, wildebeest,
impala, topi, zebra, bushbuck, roan, monkey . . .

Wild life management through manipulative &
custodial techniques, to preserve & improve
the habitat, & a soul poultice to soothe
the periodic male restlessness are, from time
to time, necessary. Tracking & bringing down
a prime specimen in its prime, feasting of its meat,
hauling home the trophy, answers both needs.

Now podium perched, sun speckling off his oval
spectacles, "The credit, " TR barks, spittle-sprays,
"belongs to the man who is actually in
the arena; whose face is marred by dust and sweat
and blood," speech-notes crumbled in his left hand, "who strives
valiantly . . ." in his voice, once snickered as "squeaky,"

retrained on the frontier & no longer elicits
'our own Oscar Wilde' references, he continues,
"who knows the great enthusiasms, the great
devotions," air pounding right fist, as if
demanding entry through an oaken door, "and spends
himself in a worthy cause; who, at best, knows
the triumph of high achievement . . ." leaning forward now,
hand gripping the rail behind the straw boaters
of note-taking reporters, "so that his place shall
never be with those cold and timid souls who know
neither victory nor defeat." The crowd, mainly
men, roars its encouragement with genuine, deep-
throated, heart-swelled appreciation.

Interlude five

Lynching. Macon County, Alabama

In the meantime, birds in a dark woods in southeastern
Alabama cease at the thrashing in the briar,
then the splashing through the shallow spring.

. . . THEM
(the good white chivalry, Christian & civilized
to the last & least)
Who's grinning now?

THEM
If you want change well, by God, we'll give you change.

HIM
Thus passes the glory of the world . . . ?

TR
". . . who errs and comes up short again and again,
because there is no effort without error or
shortcoming, but who knows the great enthusiasms . . ."

THEM
Change it right back to the way it was.

HIM
Run . . . Jump . . . Down . . . Head spins . . . Around . . .

TR
". . . the great devotions, who spends himself for a
worthy cause . . ."

THEM
Come, dance a jig, jig . . . Wheel about . . .

HIM
Stumble, wheel about . . .

TR
" . . . who, at the best, knows, in the end, the triumph
of high achievement . . ."

THEM
In control. As in control as a god: total.
Absolute. Ours: of his every fleeing step, slip,
trip, crawl. The helpless humiliation. & up
again. Running. Clumsy. All grace gone. His knowing,
evident to the trained eye, the back's contortion,
the hunched posture, the inevitability,
without possibility or redemption, but
a good sport. & God's will be done by the strict hand.

TR
". . . and who, at the worst, if he fails, at least he fails
while daring greatly, so that his place shall never
be with those cold and timid souls who knew neither
victory nor defeat."

HIM
(suspected of the usual crime)
. . . turn about . . . face them . . . their Psychosis, Lunacy,
Insanity, Sadism, Paranoia . . .

Roped.
Dragged.
Hoisted.

Body a crazy quilt: hack, gash, slash, whack, hackle,
rabbet, mangle, carve, hew, tear, cleave, skive, rive, rip, pierce,
pommel, puncture, slice, notch, lop, flay. Till each who wants
has their say.

Plip
plop.

Tries, with what there is left, to remember some tale
of—change, of changing over, crossing, like a bridge
in the dark; like sinner to Christian; season
to season; day to night; to know how it went; some
way to molt the skin of a thousand splinters of sun,
slip it off. Rise.

THEM
Yankees think we can (ever) ban the strict hand,
a tool more valuable than plow, hoe, gin, or scythe.
Fear—the deterrent. Counters chaos; terror.
A dog dancing up-right & yipping "Dixie" will,
without the sniff of the whip, rip your throat to lace.
The strict hand is the tool of orientation,
the civilized Southern's last line of defense.

Plop plop.

HIM
There are no snap-fast recollections. His mother,
Bless her soul, does not wrap him in her embracing
whisper. He does not swing buck naked from vine
into a swimming hole; foot race for a brown gal's grin,
cradle his firstborn, harvest his first crop . . . Only
a flare, beyond all convention, just in time, but
too late: Them. Before him. A congregation
of the ordinary.

THEM
A strict hand—essential for self-preservation—
wields the brand, burns Caucasian on the negroid
frontal lobe; searing the cancerous sass
from the negroid psyche.

HIM

Here, the masks of their humbled everyday are chucked
away like peanut hulls to hogs. Here, shucked of the haint
of being igged & bossed, there's no tipping on eggshells,
no hat in hand. This, here, then is the quick of the Them
they dream. This rite right here is how low they sink
seeking parity.

THEM

It is our Duty, beyond what sport & fun there
may be (& there is). It is Christian. Our legacy
to the Future. Sanctioned by the Word. The Book. Is
God's Old Testament, uncontestable law. To
not, would be wicked, wickedness of the deepest,
blackest, & most God-angering sort there is, or
could ever be. A breakdown of law and
civilized behavior.

HIM

A witness. What there is of him (left). Unclouded
by descent of darkness or rise of veiling smoke:
smells each breath, armpit, crotch, ass-crack, foot, shod or bare;
feels each quickened beat in each phlegmy throat, each twitch
& tic beneath parchment-thin skin; tastes vittles,
tobacco, snuff, & likker, brewed & store-bought in
each dry or salivating mouth; hears each of their
thoughts; sees each furrow of dirt in the creases
of each string-lean hand, neck, & face; each freckle,
wrinkle, scratch, callus, scar, scab, corn, bunion, blemish,
birthmark, & wart, & all soil, dandruff, & earwax crud
under each fingernail; & in each pitiless &
hard as a knot-hole eye, sees a refusal
to turn away, but in each, sees, inescapable,
some sacrificed but needful thing in them, shrivel
shrink, like an unwatered bloom.

Clear as crystal ice.
Inescapable.
Witnesses.
Knows.

To be shuck of the gnawing null of their human
need, even at the spiting sacrifice of saving
grace, they wait, baited, rooted in the downward suck
of blood-tainted soil. (Plip plop.) Helpless against it
as apple from limb. Under duress of a ruthless
duration of rejection & despair—their
fellow-feelings—the blighted fruit of the second
pickings of their fields, turns. The natural dis-
integration of ripe to rot drying the juice,
withering the pulp to a wizened lump
of smoldering, combustible ash. They,
in this arena, their Garden of Minstrel
Avengement, await his buck dance's last jig step,
& will root, riotous at the joyous moment
of his demise, & the rise of cold-blooded
Supremacism's hot-blooded revival
of their kinds' overcoming of renegade
prairie red featherheads; savage little brown
Mexicali greasers, Cubano Oyes,
Filipino pineapples, & big black brutes
right here in Dixie trying to ride roughshod
over our way of life.

Plip plop.

Baby crying.
Smoke, a curtain, thick as ginned cotton, lifts
into black-shrouded branches, leaves, & sky.

Flames,
like Eastern tiger swallowtails,

butterfly about him,
light,
tremor & flare,
fume.

Till at last, for him, Time, the measure of duration,
separates from Space, 3-dimensional expanse
in which all material objects are located
& all events occur, & he, in the perception
of his agony, discovers, as does Einstein,
fiddling, just about that time, with Time,
that when one's mind is right one can be—anywhere,
any time, any place. Her arms, or Jehovah's.
He, passes past or present pain, transcends.

Jumps down
spins around

        neck odd-angled,
        body a pendulum
        tolling.
        Their chorused-cheer bursts into night's disapproval.

        Hangs.

        An object
at rest tends to stay at rest
& an object in motion
tends to stay in motion
with the same speed
& in the same direction
unless acted upon
by an unbalanced force.

Baby crying.

A scream is the last he hears. Uncertain if it

is his, one of theirs, or—the near-distant whistle'd
announcement of the evening train into Tuskegee.

THEM

Laughing. Crowd in from the bookended lantern- &
torch-lit semicircle of horses, wagons, &
Them, beneath the beast, hats as various as their
wearers; Sunday go to meetings: white shirts, braces,
starched overalls, women in thin cotton, mammy-
made or mail-order, & shawls against the chill,
gangling barefoot boys in knee-britches, girls, shy, toes
curled in the dirt. Double barrels, over-n-unders,
pistols, pitchforks, pikes, staves, clubs. Chained hounds, panting.

Plip
plop.

Posed.
Smile!
Hold it—Shutter click.

Moment captured. Made permanent. Eternal.
One more!

His shoe in the dust, a hole in the toe.
Its mate up the road.

A shutter click.

Plip
plop.

Time burned into paper,
        thanks to the 1-
        dollar Kodak Brownie, affordable to all
        for preserving a moment.

—Got y'all!
—See to me getting one.
—Me too.
There'll be plenty, they're promised.

The things we have to do to do the things we have
to do. "Audemus jura nostra defendere."
"We Dare Defend Our Rights." Will replace "Here we rest"
as Alabama's state motto.

Lynching bee;
chance to catch our breath. Let off steam.
Friends with friends.
Fathers spending time with sons.
If we don't get these young'n's in it now
it'll go away.
That's what makes it all worth it, to see the smiles
on their faces, like after a Silas Green show.
Better.
Like a physic.
Only fun.
Picnic, church, holiday, hunt, last day of school,
barbecue rolled into one, & I come away
with nothing to show for it. Leastwise no keepsake.
Bob Joe got a toe bone charred black as a berry,
R. C. an ear. Reckon I learnt plenty though.
Keep my eyes open, Pa'd said. See't how it weren't
no different with quarry & a man—nigger,
I mean: flush & bring down. With a nigger it's
more sport, seeing as it's just for—souvenirs &
to send a message t'others to fear the White Man
& all such. Still I wish't I'd of got something,
seeing it is my first . . .

BT steps down onto the platform, satchel in hand.
Home. Whisper: Lynch. Local. Word: Lay low.

Notes Carver

climbing the stairs to his room . . . 15, 16, at
the creeping pace of a twinning peanut vine . . .
17, 18, 19 . . . BT walks on, walks
on, weary to the bone. *2,3,4.*

"Jim Crow, Jim Crow,
got me on the roam,
have got me on the roam."

THEM
Brownie shots while torchlight lasts. The catch. Groups
of 1 or 2. Families. Weary but restless.
Reluctant as sleepy children, part, & head for home.
Will toss & turn before they dream.

Ash, smoke, & smell, unruffled by wings of night's
black birds, linger long, long after.

Interlude
six

In Which Is Related the Aftermath, with Spiders & Webs & a Widow Mother's Planning

Hum hm h*mummm*

Baby crying.

It is still a tough time for negroes.
How long?
2, 3, 4 . . .

Crying baby.

Hum hm huum*mummm*

HER
Can't stay here can't stay here can't stay here, she says, don't
know where don't know where but can't stay here can't stay here.

Baby crying.
                How long?

Mewing son suckling her now widow's nipple,
as she, in the morning-after, eyes the dangling
twist; slow & resolute as the loop of heaven's lights.

For their idiocy to hold sway Jim Crowists,
while making us jump down spin around through the fool-
witty ether of their self-born supremacy,
think time, successive existence, is jacked back
to the dark abysm of their false-faced good ol'
Golden Days (when niggers in their place, acted up-
on by an unbalanced force, stayed in their place),

& even now can still be kept inert or at
least still be slowed to foot-dragging, bone-idle
tempo by their terrorism.

Can't stay here can't stay here, she says, *don't know where,
don't know where but can't stay here can't stay here.*

Thread by silvery thread the garden spider, black
& gold, weaves its lethal gossamer lattice.

Counseled—
        Never think that God's delays are God's
denials.—
        Consoled—
        Hold on;—
Half hears about pain's
abruptness—
        Hold fast;—
        & nature's & time's slow—
        Hold
        out.—
        but certain pace—
        Patience is genius.
        Zigging-zagging ghost bridge between tree branch &
          trunk.

She needs fleet, not forbearance; needs for time
to scurry forth like segmented spider's legs,
nimble as ragtimers' capering fingers,
capable of sparking her anger, freeing her screams,
urging running rants, tearing of flesh & hair—

How long?

Spider, done, hangs in its snare's bull's eye, awaiting.
—but if escape from these savages is simple

as that she would have taken it long, long ago.

A wasp's maddening, cocksure, rapacious whir. Darts
dazzled; webbed by dewy strings shiny as
magazine pearls. Spider, 8 limbs a-loping, greets
its flailing guest; trusses it in a silken shroud. Bites.

Grieve but plan, 's'what he'd say, she thinks.
Thinks:
*Little boy, going to try, try & get you beyond
the snap & slither of these mad-dogs & 2-faced snakes.
Try, try—if it's the last thing I do.*

*So you can be a man.
Grieve but plan . . . Grieve but plan . . .*

Chickens cluck, flap, & scatter as she crosses
the time-polished dooryard toward the slack cabin
where the grief-burdened old man, tears pooled in sightless
eyes like soapy water in an enamel washbowl,
slumps.

& still it is a hard time for negroes.
How long.

Says: *Git!*—Not just a crop life, but seasons. Clear of
the length of their lethal reach; sprout new roots to run
like spider's tendrils, shoots of new growth, like highways,
& railroads north & east & west, underground streams
tunneling through, under, & around. Away. Past.
Clear. Off. From. Afar. Elsewhither. Yonder. Beyond.

Sings: *Oh, come on boys & line the track . . .*

As the sorrow-browed hound whines its gut-deep repine.

6

Which Treats of George Washington Carver (1864-1943, Inventor, Tuskegee Professor); Invent, Inventor, Inventing & Polaris

"Discontent is the first necessity of progress."
—T. Edison.
　　　"Fear of something is at the root
of hate for others, and hate within will
eventually destroy the hater." From "Black
Leonardo," Edison's "treasured friend," George
Washington Carver.

Invent.
Inventor.
Invented.

Carver, whose greatest invention, in spite
of what you've heard, is himself.

Invent: To produce or contrive (something

previously unknown) by the use of
ingenuity or imagination.

Inventor: someone who incorporates existing
concepts or methods & modifies or transforms
them into something new.

Invented: conceived, concocted, cooked-up,
coined, forged, fabricated, hatched, minted, or
trumped-up by the imagination.

"As many more individuals of each species
are born than can possibly survive; and as,
consequently, there is a frequently recurring
struggle for existence, it follows that any being,
if it vary however slightly in any
manner profitable to itself, under
the complex and sometimes varying conditions
of life, will have a better chance of surviving,
and thus be naturally selected. From the strong
principle of inheritance, any
selected variety will tend to propagate its new
and modified form."
Charles Darwin—1859
*On the Origin of Species by Means
of Natural Selection.*

Following Edison's final lights out, the oft-
spun tale by Carver, Tuskegee professor for
2 score & 7 years, was that Edison offered
—50 or 100—or—200 thousand
dollars per annum (depending on the needs of the telling)
just to, unencumbered, do his thing.

Carver, teaming with Washington as Tuskegee Worlds'
dualistic cosmology, echoes "Learn to

do common things uncommonly well," adding
on the real side, ". . . anything that helps fill
the dinner pail is valuable." As to
methodology the "good plant doctor," flouting
scientific behavior's routines & norms,
works alone; cunningly commits nothing to paper;
when questioned proves impalpable as quicksand.

Of Edison's offer, in the tradition
of schemers far & wide, shuffles & shucks—
then declines. The anecdote proving more
profitable than the proffered position.
He holds to his Tuskegee turf, & with
the wily mother-wit of Anansi,
a.k.a., Aunt Nancy, the African spider-
trickster, who teaches mankind—*Drum roll please*—
agriculture. "If I took that money," he shyly,
slyly prats with a reflective pause, "I might forget
my people."

Be it known, a master at the game, he admits
once, "I'm not very old, but I've been around a
long time." Long enough to sow the legend of plowing
a new furrow in farming; reversing the rot
of the greed-depleted Alabama soil,
a grave for cotton seeds, sucked to a trace of the
needed trace elements: boron, chlorine, cobalt,
copper, iron, manganese, magnesium, zinc,
molybdenum, & sulfur, by soliciting
the secrets of yams, soybeans, & goobers from his God,
the Creator, who, Carver claims, speaks to him
"*through flowers, rocks, animals, plants . . .*" enabling
him to tender a needed crop-rotation plan
sans remuneration, via his inventively
discovered wizardry. & with each head-hung, tattered-
attired, shuffle-gaited retelling of his

Edison tale, each congressional hearing, each
press appearance in his "peanut man" pose, each leaflet,
each iffy add-on to his soufflé of goods presumed
puffed & fluffed from the esse of his pet plants—
                                                    strand by
strand he, slowly, patiently as peanut butter
molasses, spins a widening web of wise ol'
wooly-headed-Uncle shuck & jive.

As the needed symbol of humility,
humanitarianism, & penny-pinching,
Carver is a sedative; the non-threatening
Good Negro, the puttering Patriarch, counter
to widespread belief in inherent weakness
of the Negroid mind & spirit. & as such
sets himself as too, too exalted & cocooned
to be brought down by anything feeble
as reality. He scales, rickety-kneed,
to the upper pantheon of mythology
American style. Is, in '48, the 2d
colored man on a U.S. postage stamp.

Postage stamp glue is 1 of his vegetable
derivatives.

In '98 (year his 2d stamp is issued) is
the 1st with a USS sub named for him.
Polaris type, fully loaded, 2-staged,
solid-fueled, nuclear-powered,
ballistic warheads, the works.
                    Polaris,
polar, Earth's northern polestar; the North Star—
projection of Earth's axis—burns bright, moves,
as does Carver, so slowly that in a Muybridge
sequential photoshoot, the Tuskegee chemurgist,
in his benign hobbling, appears to be standing still.

Interlude
seven

In Which Is Related the Strange Out-of-Body Out-of-Time Encounter, with an Epigram, Stepin Fetchit, & Mach's Principle of Gravity

"De rooster chew t'backer, de hen dip snuff.
De biddy can't do it, but he struts his stuff."
—From Zora Neale Hurston's **Mules and Men** (1935)

It is a strategy
(Invent.
Inventor.
Invented.)
adapted with great
profit by Stepin Fetchit. It propels him
also to stellar stardom.

& now
a Griffitherian cross-cut:
(Invent.
Inventor.
Invented.)
to a flash forward
for a lengthy digression re Stepin Fetchit,
before returning to POLARIS:

See
the 1920s & '30s:
Close up:
Former vaudeville performer Lincoln Theodore
Monroe Andrew Perry, a.k.a. Stepin Fetchit.
b. 1902, or, slow as he is, maybe it
is really 1892. (Just below

the level of consciousness we hear a bedlam
of hounds, applause, screams of laughter, screams of pain.)

Fetchit credited with being the first feature-
billed negro in an American motion picture.
In a series of "delightful" "slices of
Americana," "period pieces," &
"family sagas," Fetchit personifies squeamish,
skittish, shiftless, mindless; a cipher (fit only
for comic & psychic relief). He is a rascal
who won't behave, but is a threat to no one.

Read this last line as (a) irony or (b)
sarcasm, or (c) both. He reportedly
makes more than a million dollars. Fetchit in
stepping to fetch *it*, or do anything else,
has mastered slow, almost no, motion.
                                    He, in his
seeming lethargy, his natural or studied
lassitude, is, perhaps, the prototype of Ernst
Mach's principle of gravity. Mach, 1838–
1916, asserts that all motion is
relative & not innate in a body.
The Austrian physicist and philosopher
hypothesizes that the inertia of a
body, any body, particularly, it
seems, Fetchit's lank & languid body, is
determined by its relation to the force(s)
of everything else around it. Thus, the "local"
behavior of the body, particularly Fetchit's,
loath to work as it is, is influenced by the
"global" properties of the universe. Thus
Perry can argue, with Mach's corroboration,
that it isn't so much he presents himself
as ignorant & lazy, but that his frame-dragging
is, considering with all due respect, Suh,

the totality of the phenomenon of
time & space in the cosmology. & that is
just the way thangs is. Maybe they is even meant
to be that way, far as he can reckon, Suh.

Whites love, are green-envious of, Stepin Fetchit.
He, as they deeply wish they could, stops Time—Oh if
they could truly do that, think how much they wouldn't
have to forget of their do-do doings & ways—

                                                    &

he is the quintessence of their idea of
stopped progress for the coloreds.

Fetchit is frozen in that make-believe belle epoch
when their romantic self-reveries peak. So, yes,
they love him even when he is ever so slightly
getting his own way, snail-wiggling, like a stripper
slow molting her sequins & feathers, out of some
make-work chore conceived to watch him snail-waggle out
of it.
        (Just below the level of consciousness
we hear a bedlam of hounds, applause, screams of laughter,
screams of pain.)

Insert film clip.
Judge Priest,
1934. Fox Film Corporation.
Written by Irvin S. Cobb about "familiar
ghosts of my own boyhood," & who says of TR, "You had to hate the
        Colonel a whole lot to keep
from loving him."

Judge Priest set in 1890 in a sleepy
Kentucky hamlet, stars Will Rogers, world-famous,
widely popular American humorist
of the vaudeville stage, called, complementarily,

the cowboy Nietzsche, by the *New York Times.*

Rogers/Priest promises chicken thief Fetchit/Jeff
(billed, 1 below Hattie McDaniel's 13th)
a *coon skin* coat [writer's emphasis] as pay for
a minor chore. Fetchit/Jeff, overjoyed at the
prospect of the discard coat, & with dozy zeal
mumbles words to that effect. Asked if he can play
"Dixie" on the harmonica he so happens
to be holding, Fetchit/Jeff *draaaaawlllllllllls* he'll play
"Dixie" or, "Marching Through Georgia," or anything
. else for dat coat.
                    Fetchit/Jeff, slyly &
Mercury-quick delivers his seemingly mindless,
but caustically signifying slip-of-the-tongue
shiv of humiliating Rebel historical
reality twixt the ribs & into the heart
of the proceedings with his "Marching Through Georgia" gibe,
i.e., his razor-sharp reference to battlin'
Billy Sherman's Savannah Campaign, capturing
Atlanta, scorching a path to the Atlantic,
& effectively breaking the economy
& spirit of the Confederacy.
                    Rogers
—his comic timing equally deft—reminds
Fetchit/Jeff he, Rogers/Priest (quote) Got him out
of one lynching, but if he catches him playing
"Marching Through Georgia," he'll join the lynching party
(unquote).
            Fetchit/Jeff, blast his lazy, unfazed bones,
hardly moving, rushes off. So thrilled in his furtive
befuddlement at the chance of the gift garment
he, with a matador's agility & grace,
sidesteps & dismisses the bull of the lynching
mention.
            (Just below the level of consciousness

we hear a bedlam of hounds, applause, screams of laughter,
screams of pain.)

Paying public whites, who, unlike Rogers/Priest, can't,
or won't, read, or hear between the lines, miss the put-
on of Fetchit's put-offs. They take the sugared swill
he serves up as the real Negro deal, sop it up
like secret formula Alaga syrup's "Sweetness
of the South." Yum yum.

Quick cross-cut in our 1915 flash forward:
hot
Southern night.
A lynching bee.
    A smidgen, towhead boy in torchlight
shimmies up the sweet-gum tree,
the rope clenched in his snaggled teeth.
      "Atta boy, Jimmy Lee!"
      "Bless his little heart."
      "Now loop the noose over the limb, honey
       . . ."
      they drawl . . .

Insert:
CHICAGO DEFENDER
Bar graphs charting Southern lynch statistics.
Insert:
Photograph:
. . . the banner outside the NAACP
office testifies in 1915 . . .

   **A MAN WAS
   LYNCHED
   YESTERDAY**

Ken Burns Effect:

... day after day Black press editorials
decrying mob murders being looked on as
lessons local laws allow.

Quick cut back to our 1915 flash forward:

THEM
... not satisfied
they cut him
down,
then
cut him
up
for keepsakes (penis,
digits, ears) ... Then
ignite him
    stumps & stem.

Stepin Fetchit living the dream lulls in
luxuries' lap; gives lavish parties; has Chinese
servants; owns 6 homes & a dozen automobiles.

Insert film clip:
    Judge Priest.
    At film's sentimental fade a tattered
    band of blacks play "Dixie," glorifying the
Confederacy vets Fetchit/Poindexter,
in coonskin coat & top hat, leads the parade,
as a babble of pickaninnies dance around
& behind.
"Lookaway, look away..."

Fade out.
Cross-cut to flashback:
c. **1901**
Look away to faraway skies through Carver's

burning eyes: *Polaris;* polar; Earth's northern polestar;
North Star projection of Earth's axis, moving,
in the distant deep, slow & burning bright as
Carver's aspirations, but well within his grasp.

(Invent.
Inventor.
Invented.)

Henry Ford (1863–1947),
master of mass production, of whom it is said,
he is like a postage stamp. He sticks to one thing
until he gets there. Is social experimenter,
& another George Washington Carver
admirer. Finances an automatic
elevator so the artful agriculturist
needn't scale the wearying 19-step flight
to this room.

& who, you perhaps wonder, is the 1st colored
on a stamp folks had to lick the back of? Carver's
cohort & Tuskegee cemetery-mate,
Booker T.; in their 2-star constellation
Sirius, the brighter light to Carver's Polaris.

Treason.
Disloyalty.
Betrayal.

Act.
Actor.
Acting.

Act.
verb
1 obsolete: actuate, animate

2 a: to represent or perform by action
especially on the stage
b: feign, simulate
c: impersonate

3: to play the part of as if in a play
4: to behave in a manner suitable to
actor.

noun
1: one that acts: doer
2 a: one who represents a character
in a dramatic production
b: a theatrical performer
c: one who behaves as if acting a part

Acting.
noun
1. The occupation of an actor or actress.
False behavior; pretense.

adjective
1: performing services temporarily

A kinked knot in 2 strings of Time; or skipped grooves
of parallel rotating tracks of cosmic
temporal measure, result in an action-at-
a-distance meeting of matter over mind, or
mind over matter. A paradox. & they, PERRY, & HER,
divided by 25 hundred miles, &
nearly 30 years, have a shared, voodoo-spooky
dream that haunts them each in their own time.

PERRY: his pre-party nap on the zebra-skinned chaise
with Habutai silk pillows.

HER: raw gal in faded dress, suckling babe at her
breast in fitful sleep on rag-pallet before dawn-
rising & rush to the fields, baby a-drag on

the sack—type he (thinks) he's left behind in Key West.
& to HER, he is tall, bald, better dressed than
any white man she's ever seen.

PERRY
I am only me. To see me in life is to
know what's on screen—foolish, mulish, meek—is a means;
me mocking their reason for needing me to be.

HER
Too modest. You're more. You are, in the eyes of
crackers who take comfort in & laugh at you,
the entire race.

PERRY
Crackers who *pay* to laugh at me.

HER
We, your own, pay more than they.

PERRY
While I laugh right back at them.

HER
—blood money in blood.

PERRY
Laugh all the way to the bank.

HER
We cut him down. I cried, all the way
to the burying ground. & back—

PERRY
I set Hollywood on fire.

HER
—weep still. There were barely his ashes to inter.

PERRY
I am the self-made artist & businessman . . .

HER
Bad business.

PERRY
What's achievable through hard work. The American Dream . . .

HER
Evil business.

PERRY
& a pioneering artist. My act will
open doors . . .

HER
Act or acquiesce?

PERRY
. . . for generations to come.

HER
They will succeed *in spite of,* not *because* of you.

PERRY
Do you know what an artist is? Does?

HER
I know what a snake is. Does.

PERRY
My name will ring because I kicked open doors

to front offices & bank vaults. Follow this now—
I am a trickster artist, like Anansi the spider.

HER
Tricking yourself.

PERRY
Scheming.

HER
2-faced, fork-tongued, double talk.

PERRY
Through humor I hiss my defiance.
My act is our anger concealed by comedy's cloak.

HER
'neath your foolery rednecks find fun to hide their fear & guilt.

PERRY
Actor's real feelings are masked.

HER
The louder they laugh at you the less they hate themselves.

PERRY
If I showed them my real face I wouldn't last a second.

HER
Truth is more than skin deep, & goes naked. Truth hates
a mask, hates a hood, hates all that tries to hide it.

PERRY
Each shuffling step, roll of my eyes . . .

HER
The betrayed grieve, but not alone.

PERRY
. . . scratch of my head, is a razor stroke 'cross their throat.
That is acting. A fool's fangs are sharper
than the wicked's.

HER
Play the fool, there or here, but I saw, & whiffed,
the finale of your fool's act played out in the woods,
where the bloodthirstys left him.

PERRY
You mistake me for somebody bent on evil.

HER
& you're innocent as babbling water over
a rock? Well, smooth-running water can hide a snake.

PERRY
It is hurtful to be called disloyal; even
when undeserved it sticks like molasses & fire.

HER
Sweet & hot as the night of my son's conception.

PERRY
See it from where I sit. I rolled the dice & up
jumped 7!

HER
Your gamble cost you your invented, treasonous,
disloyal, betraying, obsolete, feigning soul.
& it cost me my man. See it from where I sit.
You might not have looped the noose over the limb, but

as they hoisted him, hand over hand, inch by hitch,
hung him to swing bell-like to warn the rest,
your acting the fool okayed their thinking him a
nought, not a man; a cipher, with no more worth
or weight than a spider's web.

PERRY
I'm just trying to make a living.

HER
Left him charred & clothed in cobwebs. So, your fool's clothes
are covered in his blood, & you couldn't be
any more an accomplice if you'd lit their
pinewood torches.

PERRY
There's lucky & unlucky; there's having & not.
I did not write that across the heavens, but I
read it in the stars, & took it as my guide.

HER
On Satan's leash. The betrayer, for gain of goods
or ease, treads threads of his own sticky, silken web
of deceiving, & will die, blue, broke, demeaned, coiled
in loops of woe of his own weaving. That is
reality.

PERRY
Hollywood is farther from Key West than most
Negroes can think, let alone traverse & conquer.
But Lincoln Theodore Monroe Andrew Perry
found the way. I am a star. Unique. Singular.

HER
I say it to your double face, you will fall
like Lucifer from your Hollywood heaven, &
plummet down into a Judas's hell.

PERRY

Though, like the tortoise they liken me to, I have grown
a thickened shell, still your words find their way to wound.

HER

If I prayed I'd pray 2 things: that before the rope's
jerk, or flame's flicker, they glimpsed the measure of the man
he was, & they were not—

PERRY

—&—?

HER

At your dying breath you do too. Justice will serve
what's deserved. On my man's soul I hope you die
alone & hungry.

PERRY

I must bathe & dress for my evening's soiree.
A registry of Hollywood elites will attend.
I am, even amongst their stellar constellation,
the most distinct & distinguishable. Without
discernable movement or spent energy I
am as firmly fixed in their astrological cluster
as the moon, the sun, or the Northern Star.

HER

Puff your chest & crow to your own light,
but the betrayer's fate will twist your neck,
& pluck you, & drop you, plop, in Hell's pot, where
you will boil till the last light of heaven fades.

PERRY on awakening stretches, yawns, wonders
why he had a dream like that; blames the late lunch brisket,
rings for Xiong, & a Puritan, gin with Noilly Prat,
shaken, with orange bitters & a dash of Yellow
Chartreuse.

HER cuticles bloody she reaches a handful
back into the sack. Drags a step forward.

Polaris; polar; Earth's northern polestar;
North Star projection of Earth's axis, moving,
in the distant deep, slow & burning bright.

(Just below the level of consciousness we hear
a bedlam
of hounds, applause, screams of laughter, screams of pain.)

Treason.
Disloyalty.
Betrayal.

Act.
Actor.
Acting.

Invent.
Inventor.
Invented.

Interlude
eight

Polaris; Newton's Laws 1–3; Lynching; Migration; On Uses of the Blues

Think back:
              Say a couple hundred years. Say 2
hundred 14 to be exact. Cambridge, England,
University of Cambridge, Trinity College.
1687. The desk of Isaac Newton
(1643–1727).
Straight up, flat out, no doubt physiological,
mathematical, anthropological,
philosophical, alchemical,
theological genius.
                    To be Sir (—how much
thought had to go into that?).

Read over his shoulder. His *Philosophiae
Naturalis Principia Mathematica.*
It lays the groundwork & clears the path for a world
of knowing the basic hows & whys. Thumb through to
the classic mechanics section. Packed with stuff
about universal gravitation & the
3 laws of motion explaining why objects move
(or don't) as they do. & how the same natural
laws govern the movement of objects on Earth &
those of the heavenly bodies.
                            (& giving lie
to the assertion of the earth being Anglo-
centric rather than Heliocentric.)

Newton's 1st Law: of inertia:
                        Says simply, more
or less, every body

       (&/or everybody,
including, the, until very recently, by
law enslaved ((by recently, Oh, say can you see
3 decades & 6 or so—a more exact number
of the ending of that unnatural state of
being, or baring, depends on how 1
calculates the state of affairs of states' states of
mind (((specific locale, judicial &
jurisdictional discretion, &c,
&c, being so variable being
more exact is mathematically &
theoretically difficult—)))
                 perseveres in
its state of moving, or not moving,
                 (including,
in the case of the above-mentioned multitude,
often having to make a way out of no way),
except insofar as it is compelled to change
its state
       (state of residence, &/or state of mind)
by **an unbalanced force.** (Author's emphasis.)

Before we recap think:
Lynchings
Jim Crow
Boll weevils
Droughts

—Hands? Yes.
—Let me see if I can break it down. If something out
of balance ain't going nowhere, it's going to keep on
going nowhere until something makes it.
—Correct.
—& something that is going somewhere, it'll keep
doing it at the same speed until something else,
maybe the first thing in the first place, speeds it up.

—Right again. These are the simplest reasons bodies
or somebody's move.
—Rock on.

Lynchings
Jim Crow
Boll weevils
Droughts

Lynchings
Jim Crow
Boll weevils
Droughts

2d Law.
2 things determine the speed of the moving body
(or bodies):
the force of the mover, & its size.

Lynchings
Jim Crow
Boll weevils
Droughts

The 3d Law, Newton essentially says, is that
the response to every action is a reaction
that is equal, in size, and opposite, in
direction.

Lynchings
Jim Crow
Boll weevils
Droughts

&/so, finally, even in the South,
given the perfect tempest of lynchings, Jim Crow,

boll weevils, & droughts, the laws of nature, &
the (Jim Crow) laws of man are no longer
separate, but in contentious alliance &
equal in their force on the negro body, or
the body of negroes. Push has come to shove.

Correct. Mass migration begins.

Can't stay here—

Uses of the blues:

Go down deep & stay long; walk moonlight; be that
crooked road out of the woods; lighten hardships &
fill hungry days; shift loads; get business straight; pick up
the pushed down; heed the call when things go wrong;
find lost minds; tear into foolishness like a mad dog
at a rat in a lightning storm.

Of the Migration Blues, Ship of Fools & State, & Moving on Up with Moving on Up

&/so,
to a soundtrack of the long-brewing, rapidly
coalescing blues, as yet not worthy of note,
blue or otherwise, by print-culture scribes—for of
what use can it be to them, they think, if they
even think about it, what use have they of a
lifeboat, when their strong & great Ship of State skimming
on bright waves, smooth sailing ahead, is captained,
they think, by an enlightened & caring hand.

&/so, standing, ear turned from the prevailing wind,
on what feels a solid deck, Southerners, in their
presumptions, feel no need for faith o'er fears,
"In spite of rock and tempest's roar," it is only
amongst a few below: women & the weak: poor &
powerless: praters, star-gazers; good-for-nothings
who know the blues.

&/so any regard of blues as motivator
& healer is "off-the-record" so to say. &

thus, as such, according to the gatekeepers,
the St. Peters of Official-only-what's-
written-down-or-up-&-therefore-available-
to-the-literate-exists-History, the blues, though right there,
proclaiming its verities like hammers ringing
on anvils—do not, repeat, do not exist—
to that ship of fools, other than as just more-back-
of-the-barn darky genus gibberish, you know,
with the rest of the ". . . queer goings on in the
Negro quarters," but it's the blues' ability
& intent to change & errant course from "false light
on the shore" & the thing it is named for *is*
known to those where & by whom it is needed—those
with old but newly revealed attitudes &
broadening senses of latitudes—

   Can't stay here, can't stay here—
                       & used
for the purpose that it needs to satisfy—
the telling of earthy earthly truths, rousing their
black butts, &/by keeping up their defenses
while back-paddling from the anti-humane
tradition-of-its-time bull-shit; the Aryan
chuckleheaded maintain-the-purity-of-blood-
lines hokum, that chokes the air & clouds out the light,
like ravenous, swarming locusts according to
its kind, devouring everything in their path,
as if it is their destiny manifested,
& for 300 + years the land, & those who work it,
languish & yearn under the abomination
of the land-grabber's dark night plague. Until—
                        How Long?—
finally there is a climate change, winged in
on the perfect tempest's wind; a dawning,
articulated by the blues to & for
the people for whom it is neither a question

nor a mystery, but as plain as their hair, or
lips, or noses on their faces; & the blues foretells
of an end-time from the *Wonderland* Duchess's
mad logic of, *"There's a large mustard-mine near here.*
And the moral of that is—The more there is of mine,
the less there is of yours."
                         Oh, Yes, it is still
a tough time for negroes, but haven't they cleared
the land, laid the foundation, put up the structures,
plowed, sowed, & reaped, nursed & nurtured the nation
of swaggering, nattering, 2-faced frauds,
affording them, without thanks or compensation,
the leisure to dream, think & thieve, & believe—*Their*
negroes—who only they understand & who
understand their place & love being barefoot,
hamstrung, & country—are, still, as they have been
all along—satisfied.

                         An object
at rest tends to stay at rest
& an object in motion
tends to stay in motion
with the same speed
& in the same direction
unless acted upon
by an unbalanced force.

But,
"Restlessness is discontent and discontent is
the first necessity of progress," says T.
Edison. "Show me a thoroughly satisfied
man and I will show you a failure."

&, well, McKinley Morganfield immersed in the
muddy waters of the blues finds he could *never* be
satisfied, & just can't keep from crying. &

poor Robert Johnson knows he'd been mistreated &
he's got to the place where he doesn't mind dying.
He woke up feeling 'round for his shoes. & you know
by that he has the old walking blues. But Big
Bill Broonzy, who has the key to the highway,
is bound to go, but has to leave there running,
'cause walking is much too slow.

"Be courageous! Have faith! Go Forward!" Edison again.

John Henry, steel-driving man, altogether
missing the point, tries some boss-sanctioned
labor therapy to cure what ails him, hoping
to outwork a machine.

Countering that notion totally,
"Take this old hammer,
man, take it to the captain,"
as Time & Space Aeronautical Physicist,
& African American Oral Historian,
Dr. Lead Belly, a.k.a. Huddie William Ledbetter
(1888–1949), put it,
"Tell him I'm goin', tell him I'm gone."
Goin'—gone!
& adding a scooch of Igbo lore concludes:
"If he asks you, was I runnin',
If he asks you, was I runnin',
Tell him I was flyin',
man tell him I was flyin'."

Puff!—Pow!

& once the signifying notes & chords & cries
of their bluesmen & funkybutt, honkytonk
musicianers make plain that the crumbled kingdom's

doors are ajar, their feet, itchy with discontent,
are ready for the rails or the road.

Puff!—Pow!

Boogadeeboogadee. Hightailing out from down there
like water from a bottom-busted bucket.
Even those who can't immediately gittyup
& get gone, get to vamping until it is
their time to *ALL ABOARD!*

Many 1000s go(ne).

Interlude
nine

In Which Is Related the Adventure of W.E.B. Following the Strands of the Blues through the Maze of Elitism & into Radicalization

Mean-
while, Over There: Gauguin, Strindberg, Ravel, &
Mann are busy, changing, making new,
as Sousa's sorry band, as the best America
has to offer, tours Europe with its same old
OOMPAHOOMPAHOOMPAH.
Mean-
while over here Du Bois, overhears the plaintive,
previously unheard wails & groans of black folk(s') songs.
&, way uppity from where he is, the blues'
mama & daddy, Sorrow Songs as he dubs them,
are "Weird old songs" to his elite New England ear,
"that stirred him strangely."
The most original and beautiful expression
of human life and longing yet born on
American soil," he says in *Souls of Black Folk.*
Nailing it. Made by "black folk of primitive type,"
whose "appearance was uncouth," to his elite
New England eye, "their language funny," low down.
A tribe exotic to him as Dutchmen to
Ashanti. Speaking longing & discontent as pointed
as new barbed wire, dark as minor key harmonies
of the devil's choir, & in pictures plain as sunset.
". . . the most beautiful expression of human
experience born this side the seas." Leading
him to echo the clarifying, defiant cry
at the core of the blues—a learned call, on the social
& political fronts, for understanding &
due compensation, recognition &
appreciation.

Tain't easy for brother W.E.B.
to reach down & strum those dark chords, is in fact
a life-long struggle; has a heap of advantage
to overcome before he gets his mind right & tight.

"I never failed once. It is just a 2000-
step process." (Edison.) & it is the blues,
"the greatest gift of the Negro people," which has
always been there, even from way back before, when
it is as formless as faith, that gives insight
to the bourgeois-blinded Du Bois & clarifies,
if not all the way, clears his solution-seeking course.

Puff!—Pow!

Many 1000s go(ne).

& still it is a hard time for negroes.

Of a Booker T. Ditty,
& an Imagined Want Ad

He is the head, he is the leader,
Booker T. Washington is his name.
Oh, he is the head, the leader,
Booker T. Washington is his name, Yes it is.
He stands for us, he speaks for us,
No-body else can make that claim.
(Repeat above.)

✻ **WANT AD** ✻

WANTED: *New Leader*
for the Negro People.

DUTIES: 1. Explore & implement strategies to stop the gradual erosion of the rights of the Colored in continuing decline since Reconstruction. 2. Counter-act the accommodation to the betrayal of our hope from without & within. 3. Plot the path to economic & social rights, i.e., 1st class citizenship.

QUALIFICATIONS: To graduate from studying Negroes to prove (to those who don't care) they can be more than sweat & strain Negroes, to leading them. Willing to go through a series of wrenching revelations about ever-increasing radical possibilities.

5–8 YEAR STRATEGY:

———————————

Scale down from the tower; organize a trip to the scenic North, co-found a politically active group. Demand attention from business, scholars, churches, society, & history. Specific duties: Be Queequeg. Harpoon the ghosty Tuskegee leviathan, bulling its space-displacing bulk & spouting bilge through its blowhole. Be the author of Souls of Black-folk. No others need apply.

Contact,

WILLIAM MONROE TROTTER,

Co-founder

Boston Guardian

———————————

In Which Is Related the Unfortunate Adventure That Befalls Booker T. When He Encounters Certain Wicked Upstarts in Boston

Tip.
Tilt.
Churn.
Churn.

THE BOSTON RIOT

Dramatis persona:

Booker T. Washington, a.k.a. BT,
a.k.a. the Wizard

William Monroe Trotter (1872–
1934), Harvard *magna cum laude;*
newspaper editor of *The Guardian,* purposed
to spread "propaganda against discrimination."
Wears 1 face.

No penchant for patience. No time for locked or
½-step takers. Too intense to tamper his temper,
bank his belly fire, tame his tongue, kowtow
to concessions of now. No agility,
ability, or care to conceal the who, what,
& how of his dapper self, or his clear seeing
of the was, is, & will be of his race. Is fraught,
frightening to those most needful of that ire, but
who are so shunted to the precipice-edge
as to shun all but most modest disruption in their name.

Knows a buffer is his need. 1, who in his blackness
is less fearsome-hot; better at suffering fools,
black or white, who trumpet or allow impositions,
idiocies, & inanities of race
as standard, reason, or excuse. A cooler, less
abrasive, more evasive sorghum-soaked tongue
to prescribe doses of system-purging draughts
served in honey-lined spoonfuls. 1, who, unlike himself,
won't, by his ferocity, blot the cause he
advocates.

Picture:
30 July '03
Boston. National Negro Business League Meeting,
Columbus Avenue (colored) Zion Church.

BT featured speaker.

Trotter's passion bursts in the middle of the meeting
in the middle of BT's speech; rises
in the middle of the church, stands in the middle
of his seat, &, in that holy place, baits the
Tuskegee bear, tugs its tail; challenges BT
to his face(!)

Hushed, they crane, gape as Trotter probes BT's pallid
policies & vanilla gripes against Jim Crow.
Demands clarity on the economics of
BT's encouraging white's notions of needy,
pleading, need-to-know-no-more-than-needed, negroes.

Calls & counter calls for him to sit; for order;
to remember where they are. Trotter egged on
in his opening salvo, BT's side claims, by
"a gang of dissolute & drunken women from
the streets" (including Trotter's sister in that
calculated slur) brought in to drown out
their leader's voice.

Let him speak.
We came to hear *him* speak.
Then let him answer.
We have the floor.
Not any more.
You have no right to question him.
We're all equals here.
Speak.
Answer.

Silence from him who, through it all, stands, portrait of
the temperance & decorum his philosophy
espouses: "regal" by his acolyte's account,
"beyond reproach," "rigid," "mortified," by those less
enamored. But stands, 5 foot, 6 inch, 1 hundred
76 lb colored Colossus 'neath Zion's
cross, body at preacher-ease, but lips a line, jaws
a vice, eyes active as if tracking the half-dart-
half-drowse of a July fly, lighting on all but
his confronter, accuser, his Judas atop
a chair—like he was raised by apes.

Out of sight on the podium's top, BT's fist,
like the gnarled knob of a cudgel, rests. Inward feels—
alimentary unease—as when suspended
atop Chicago's Columbian Exposition
Ferris Wheel ride in '93, hanging, like . . . like
spoiling fruit in the cage-like car, at the pinnacle
of Applied Science's 19th century's
possibility. 2hundred50+feet
above the blinding bright site of its creator's
self-entitled White City. Promising foreboding,
machine-run utopias from which he & his
people, bereaved & barren, would be exiled
at the farthest horizon.
                                    Tittering . . .
like a rock-a-by-baby at the tree top, till,
the startling jerk, & the device began closing
the circle of its descent; the ratcheting
click-clicking of its wheel's driving-chain; a cranking
counter-point to echoing sling stone-like runnel,
clicking & tap-tapping down his spine's icy
tunnel to the gutter of his roiling gut.
                                    Churn, churn.

At last, John Law arrives, is put upon by those
aforementioned Trotter supporters, kinswomen,
a phalanx of hatpin-poking, pocketbook-
swinging furies—till at last, order, of a kind,
is imposed.
              Still, unrest, roused like a guard dog
from its deep sleep, will not heel even as BT,
outwardly composed as if there's been no more
than a hiccup's or blink's delay, continues his
folksy anecdotes, makes his much-made, oft-heard points.

But there is more. Oh, brother, is there more.
The evening's assembly of Negroes

in Columbus Avenue Zion bear witness
to rows & recriminations long buried un-
earthed, & non-attendees, concerned whites included,
will, as word expulses like a sneeze on a gale's wings,
soon know of it.

Trotter is arrested, "taken out . . . in handcuffs,
yelling like a baby," BT reports, &
at BT's cronies' & mammets' insistence, is charged.

BT, the Afro-American establishment.
The Machine. Hook in every pond; in every race
a horse; Fido in every fight, assumes the public's
ignorance of, or indifference to, the whole affair.
After all, Trotter is nothing at all to most, he,
BT, everything to many. When he walks in
& takes a seat he guarantees his speaking is
for a solid & steady, mute & mannered bloc.

But Puss is out the bag. Dobbins out door.

Hum hm h*mummm*
2-3
Hum hm huum***mummm***

Churn. Churn.

The inner-racial nature of the episode
agitates the waters, rocks the sturdy, long-
seasoned & weather-tested vessel of BT's
appeasing creed.

Is labeled by Press & word of mouth, "The Boston
Riot."

BT feels his & his tight ship's reputation,

previously unsinkable, in a tempest.

Fears word of the incident might, where there's been no
previous doubt, stir a storm, send breakers of un-
certainty—regarding their monies' worth—seeping
over levees, through cracks & chinks into ports
in which he seeks continued safe mooring.

                              Like a
lightning-jolted compass, the needle jerks, waver-
wags from BT's once-unswerving course. The Wizard,
as if adrift on a nigger-rigged raft in cold,
roiling waters, feels irregular spasms from nape
to coccyx, stem to stern.

Churn.
Plip.

Grieves him to his heart. New-to-the-game scholar-
scoundrels. Nerve of them. Lacking, like coarse blues singers,
the caution of faith. Rush-ranting into a doomed
future. Dare throw down a public gauntlet.

                              His
allied forces, sensing their place, do his bidding,
force Trotter's conviction. 30 days, Charles Street jail.

BT pens his personal regrets to TR
for any & all discomfort or concern (not
to mention doubt) the inner-family dirty
laundry washing may have caused *him*.

But it is their audacity, this militant
clique of unannointed, unappointed freeborn,
high-yellow college-boy elites, tilts BT
to a rare, emotion-fueled, over-reactive lapse.

Churn. Churn.

Plop.

> *Waters risin', levees crumblin' down,*
> *Big water rising, levees washing down.*
> *People hollering "What can we do?"*
> *Holler & crying, "What can we do?"*
> *Moses tells 'em, "Follow me,*
> *& I will lead you through."*

Churn.

BT
A squall of missive reminders: favors granted,
deeds done, monies funneled, dictated, Personal
and Confidential, on sheaves of Tuskegee
letterhead with hints it is the know-it-all Du Bois;
who does not walk with them; the egghead who blasphemed
him in that *Souls of Black Folk;* who had, only a
few weeks before the dastardly Boston ambush,
dined at BT's table at the Oaks; is behind
the underhanded, callithumpian attack.
Signed Yours truly, sealed, sent (the Institute has
its own postmark), near & far.

Newton's 3d: the response of every action is
a reaction that is =, in size, &
opposite, in direction.

BT's over-reactive (mis)handling of the
scandale neger: taking the bait, throwing his weight;
is the final tap that tips W.E.B.
farther from Washington's humbling way of anti-
self-assertion, & dependence on moneyed
Southern whites.

Trotter, sentence served, emerges martyred. Bolstered.

Buttressed. BT's reaction, & Du Bois's
attraction to his side, was Trotter's true intention
from the first.

Each camp's faithful called to order. Noses counted,
pulses & temperatures checked, longitudes &
latitudes, lines of demarcation mapped. Put up
or stand down time.

Actions & counter-offensives, correspondence,
editorials, speeches, whispers follow: fester
into fresh accusations, innuendo,
public & private, are cast back & forth like
catapulted or slingshot stones.

> He be busy as a bee,
> but end up standing still.
> Bumblebee busy, but Timelocked,
> so he standing still.
> Can't fly from the past
> Don't believe he ever will.
> Going to end up last
> 'cause it's after
> when he think it is.
> Way, way after he thinks it is.

Churn, churn.
Churn.

TROTTER:
As advisor to 2 presidents, BT's word
has yet to null an enacted inequity,
or wrest wretched rope from tickled pink red neck
lynchers' grips.

BT:
What have they done?

What do they want?
Who do they want it for?

TROTTER:
BT, bought with hush-money from Dixie gentry's
small change, is the mute-mouth rubberstamp for lily-
white government policies. Tuskegee is
the sump into which the spoils of his bootlicking
cup-rattling is sucked.

BT:
Pestiferous, matriculated, color-struck
popinjay pretenders, clucking heritage, crowing
lineage, as if their veins, plain through pasty skin
as bottled bluing, bodes a deeper, richer lode,
& approves them plotters of our ensuing path.

Trotter from his mother, in the succession
of Hemings who claim Thom Jefferson blood.
Du Bois boasting Dutch, French, & African. His lines'
freedom bought by their great-granddaddy's soldiering
in the Revolutionary War.

While his (BT's) line, no longer than the shortest
distance between him & his nameless, faceless white sire,
wonders, in snapped remembrances & flashing clicks,
whether his *pater* (non)*familius* fox-crept,
or cock-strutted pass sty's swineslops when entering
the quarters to steal a treat, Jane, darker than
a berry, sweeter than watermelon?

Churn.

> *Nothing but a mutt,*
> *No if & or but.*
> *Ain't nothing but a mutt,*

No if & or but.
Common as tits on a milkcow.
Nothing about me highbrow,
I proclaim it near & far.
Nothing but a mutt,
Same as all my people are.

BT:
Circling like scavengers, the Trotter-Du Bois pack;
fraternity of unbent backs & uncalloused hands,
convene ill-advised forums, fashion slapdash
movements, issue resolutions & foolhardy
manifestos, but for all the scholar-scoundrels'
breeding & book-learning they can't raise a dime, while
I father a generation, make a monthly
payroll, & upkeep an institution worth 2
million United States of American dollars.

Churn.

He's a begging man,
Beg everywhere he can.
Say, he's a begging man,
Beg everything he can.
Beg from the villain, beg from the rich,

He'll beg from any ol' son'bitch.
Beg from the good guy, beg from the villain,
Beg the eggs from a setter,
Beg the seed from a watermelon.
Beg so hard for his begging self,
Leave nothing for no-body else.
Leave nothing for no-body else.
You know he's a begging man.

Churn, churn.

TROTTER/W.E.B.:
Owners & robber barons with whom Citizen
Washington guests & sups grant, through Alabama's
legislature, a lifetime free to vote voucher,
making him, of the 8hundred27
thousand + coloreds in Alabama, 1
of the less than 1thousand not recently
ballot-box banned.
        &, Yes, we are convinced his
'95 Atlanta appeasement speech tilted
the balance t'ward, & set the tone for '96's
evilly iniquitous *Plessy v.*
Ferguson's "sep'rate but equal" disaster &
all it's wrecked in its wretched wake. Washington
was, W.E.B. said, "leading the way backward."

Strong clouts that would have taken out any other,
but, no, no the champ's wobbled to the ropes, but not
floored by the blows, & what it shows—he can be hit—
in a frame-by-frame series of Muybridge-like
motion studies—his head snaps back, a feathered arc
of sweat splays like flushed quail. The blow, like a blast
in a coal seam, discharges lumps, chunks, & fragments
of qualms & scorn, breaking his rhythm, making him
cover up, clinch against the after-rumble
of body shots, & fight for vamping time to clear
his head—but still on his feet. In the scrap.

"... say,
I'll load more on you, more than you can stand,
more than you can stand.
... load it, I'll stand it like a man,
yes, I'll stand it like a man."

& yes, History shows he, a pro, no question,
shakes it off. But ringsiders who've put sure money
on a cinch—a Wonder Boy—tense.

                             Has the scrim parted
on the Tuskegee Wizard? Parted & ripped. Drip.
Has he had his hole card peeped, his ticket punched?

They lean forward, make note—flaws they've maybe ignored:
slow of foot; belly soft; iffy conditioning;
leaves his jab out a tad too long . . . small stuff many
amateurs may miss, but not smart-money's trained eye . . .

Maybe he ain't so big,
just tall that's all . . .

. . . maybe Newton's 3d
is being heard . . .

Churn. Churn.
Churn.

Hum hm h*mummm*
2-3
Hum hm huum***mummm***

Churn.

Tip.

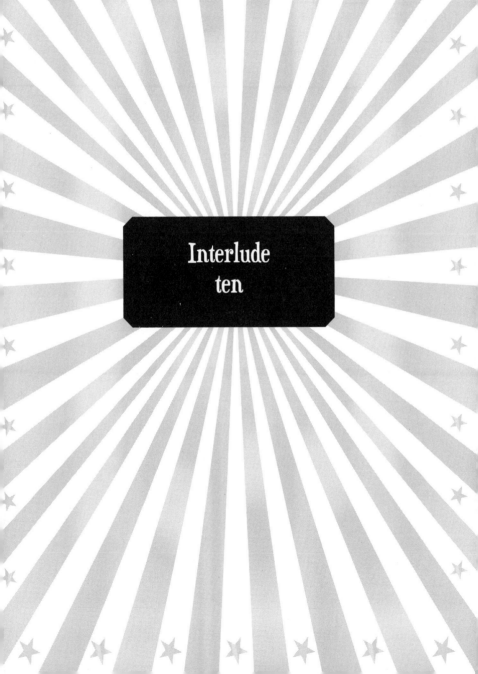

Interlude
ten

Of Tip, Tilt, Topple

Tip.
transitive verb tipped, tipping tip'·ping
to strike lightly and sharply; tip
to give a small present of money
(to a waiter, porter, etc.) for some service
to give secret information to in an attempt
to be helpful.

Tilt.
transitive verb
to cause to slope or slant; tip
to poise or thrust (a lance) in or as in a tilt
to charge at (one's opponent) in a tilt
to forge or hammer with a tilt hammer
to direct (a discussion, policy, etc.)
so as to favor a particular opinion or side

Topple.
intransitive verb
to fall (over) because or as if top-heavy
to lean forward as if on the point of falling;
overbalance; totter.
transitive verb
to cause to topple; overturn
to overthrow, to topple a monarch.

On Niagara Falls, Brownsville, Atlanta, & Newton's 3rd Revisited, + TIP & TILT

Tip.

1905.
June.
Booker T.'s ever-same policy of lip-locked
silence on ever-more eroding civil rights,
& his sucking up, like a pneumatic vacuum
cleaner, of major philanthropic funds, drives Du Bois
& Trotter + 24 men & a boy to beat
a retreat to Fort Erie, the Canadian side,
near the thunderous Falls. They confer; plot, proclaim
themselves the Niagara Movement; declare
satisfaction with no less than "full manhood rights,"
issue militant, anti-racist, anti-BT
manifestos. They pose: composed, dandied,
dignified as judges; aware it is theirs, they
eye the future full in its face. Du Bois, centered,
looking another way, weighs ways to damn to a
trickle the damned torrential racist downpour, &

ponders means to choke BT's slush to a drip.

At Washington's insistence, most white & black press
& rank & file fall in line, don't pay much mind.

                                                       But
dominos once tipped, will tilt, will, in rapid
succession, topple.

e.g.:
Brownsville.
e.g.:
Atlanta.

        The response to every action is a reaction
        that is =, in size, & opposite, in
        direction.

Brownsville, TX. An army-related incident:
black infantry troops (mis)treated with Lone Star State
(in)hospitality: reports of a raid (with spicy-dicey rumors
of an assaulted white woman plopped in the pot),
riot, & the fact of a wounded law man, &
a dead white man. TR, acruise aboard the
Presidential yacht, *USS Sylph,* his private part
of the Great White Fleet, hears of the fracas, on word
no more trustworthy than the mythological,
invisible beings fancied to inhabit
the air, & for which his leisure-time vessel
is named. Mad dog mad TR summarily dis-
charges "without honor" or possibility
of pensions, 3 companies of black soldiers. Black
soldiers, "Fighting on arrival, fighting for
survival," Robert Nesta "Bob" Marley, 19-
45–81, Rasta wailer sings, Black
soldiers, "Woy yoy yoy yoy," with
Congressional Medals of Honor, of the same

25th Regiment who, at San Juan Hill,
protected TR's macho-juiced stumbling, bumbling,
ambushed Rough Rider's rear; "Woy yoy," saved his crack
unit's bacon; plucked his big stick wielding cow-boy's
chestnuts from the fire. "Woy yoy yoy yoy!"

"A man who is good enough to shed his blood
for the country," TR says, "is good enough
to be given a square deal afterwards."
                                                    But
when it is time to put up or shut up, he puts
down & shuts out. Barking that some of the soldiers,
without hearing or trial, "should be hung," their being,
as he imagined them "bloody butchers."

"We must treat each man on his worth and merits
as a man. We must see that each is given
a square deal, because he is entitled to
no more and should receive no less," he also says.
He also says of Brownsville, "I feel the most
profound indifference to any attack which
can be made on me in this matter." So there.

Du Bois, aware of the Bull Moose–Wizard's link,
ties him to BT's tail like a tin can to a cat's.
Says, "Theodore Roosevelt does not like black folks."
Signifies: "He has no faith in them. I do not
think he really ever knew a colored man
intimately as a friend."
                            Points out, with BT
his advisor on such things, TR appointed
fewer coloreds, did he, to federal slots
than did the Napoleon of Protection,
McKinley before him.

Back in '03,
        a couple weeks post the demise
of Cassius Marcellus Clay, American
emancipationist (b. 1810),
            (not
Muhammad Ali, b. 1942, a.k.a.
Cassius Marcellus Clay, Jr., Heavyweight;
& "Greatest of all time"),
                TR, back then, days within
BT's Boston Riot, in an unrelated
matter of state, called Columbians of South A-
merica "dagos," & "contemptible little
creatures," "homicidal corruptionists," & "cat-
rabbits." Another time & circumstance, said, "It
is of incalculable importance that A-
merica, Australia, & Siberia
should pass out of the hands of their red, black, and
yellow owners, and become the heritage of
the dominant world races." & bellicose
specifically about the blacks among their number
being "altogether inferior to the whites."

& now, '05 at Tuskegee, TR, atop
a cotton bale dais, top hat in hand, preaches
patience & persistence, & the showing of thrift,
perseverance, & self-control. Coloreds' fate
being in their own hands, he says. Remarks, as if
written by BT who TR believes the best
(black or white) the South has to offer. Regarding
W.E.B. thinks & says elsewhere he is
dangerous, warns good & true negroes against him.

The colored rank & file, & schooled leadership,
further tip against BT.

Newton's 2d: The speed of a moving body
is determined by the force of the mover, &
its size.

Now come the Atlanta Riots.

Cotton prices & colored census fall, & at
their most fearful of black success white-collars &
rednecks, in feral, bestial, brute, rabid,
crazed cahoots, revive Billy Sherman's tactics: scorch
a path: maraud, maim, murder intending to
snap & sap the economy & spirit
of Georgia's capital's capitalistically
inclined coloreds. TR, who'll get the Nobel Peace Prize
for helping Russia & Japan see eye to eye,
is silent on the Atlanta occurrences
& others of a like nature. Condemns not.

Negroes once Party of Lincoln loyalists, now
with no redress, fume. Unrest festers. They too tilt.

Drip.

Tip.
Tilt.

Flashback c. 1903. Which Treats of Hollywood's 1st Flicker; Seeking Freedom; Opposites Attracting; Fair Usage; Uncle Tom; Syncretism; & Attempted Unions

Americans—i.e., bourgeoisie whites for whom,
to their chagrin, it has not all been a total
love-in—*it* being the grab & claim: the making of
a nation via conquests & checkbook
annexation of *Others* bested, all blameless,
under the shameless name of the U.S.'s
Destiny Manifested; the *all* being
the dissatisfied some, seeking release from
the beastly realization of hypocrisy
of, as Mark Twain puts it, "the moral splendor
of our high and holy civilization[s]"
imposed persuasion on red, black, & brown folks
doing just fine up till time of America's
interest & invasion.

     The sense, by said ingrate
bourgeoisie malcontents, that since the inevitable

fulfillment of His will started, inexplicably
part of their partisan spirit departed,
leaving them with a downhearted ennui, which
with hindsight we see was nothing but the blues;
prompting their seeking a guilt-freeing, personal,
& communal-reviving change of pace, &
saving of face from the ever-accelerating
new; maybe a chance to dance, as if a dark-townish
romp & stomp will jar the nuisance of burdensome,
privileged propriety from their backs & brows,
& they can gorge on immodest joys sirens sing
in their public play-praising songs, as if—if they
overexert & sweat like the new colonized
& bottom workers on the rise they will slip
the bounds of being lashed to the mast of their
polite & comfy; as if a prancing rout,
not *with,* but at least *to* devil music will absolve
their doubting, profiting body & souls
about their country's imperialistic goals.

This as 2billion dollars per is about
to be made on sheet music. Much of it negro
sourced, inspired, or associated.
                              This, as,
Big Bucks: the backers, bankers, brokers; smart money,
their steady hand in the till & on the tiller,
who sign the checks & weekend at beach houses, or
upstate estates, or down on a Southern coast. Them.
Sitting in the box seat big chair, deciding if
or when & when where who & how much, as lions
& gladiators of commerce & governance
tussle in the Coliseum of commerce, &
yea, or nay as the final say, miss the boat as
on the left coast the good ship Hollywood is launched
by former captains of rags & junk.

Out East Money sneers, snipes—moving pictures! Just feed
for the trough of amusement from which the
rag & a penny sops slop.
                              Moving pictures, Ha-Ha.
Leave the bohunk, dago, heeb, kraut, paddy, polock
marginal diversions to the slavering, mongrel,
shinny-men (with their noses, Ha Ha, for rubbish).
Leave them, & the women(!) they let do it, to it,
for the fad it is, a shining bob soon to fade,
& good riddance. We, for Christ's sake, will bond with Big
Money, the sure, rock-solid bet . . .

The first time a negro is portrayed on film
a white man in blackface being *Uncle Tom's Cabin*'s
title character is it.

& Mark Twain, still not over the upshot of the
Spanish-American War's draw-down, continues
his crusade against the U.S. military's
campaign of atrocities, the water torture
of a Filipino priest being a point of note.

12

Of Use, Used; *The Clansman;* Interacting Entities & Denial of Influences; Berlin; Picasso; Abbott & Costello; & the Loas Showing Up

ALEMBIC:
A device that purifies or alters by
a process comparable to distillation.

1905.
*The Clansman: An Historical Romance of the
Ku Klux Klan*, a re-visionist novel of Re-
construction, is the South's comeback to *Uncle Tom's
Cabin.* It is a praise song to the Ku Klux Klan.
Its author is Thomas Dixon, Jr. (18-
64–1946): Scotch-Irish
Presbyterian Son of the South. Mammy-raised.
Moralist. Minister. Believes in Race Purity;
Conservative God-Fearing Values; Southern White
Womanhood's Sanctity; The Family. Believes
in Democracy; Jews' nobility; believes

in the humanism of Catholics; believes
in Abolitionist William Lloyd Garrison's
defiant stance against all odds; believes negroes
"kindly, patient, humorous"; believes in Anglo-
Saxon Superiority; & negro in-
feriority. Preaches Domination or
Separation. Dedicates his novel, to his
uncle, North Carolinian "Scotch-Irish
leader of the South . . . Grand Titan of the Ku Klux Klan."

Of *Clansman* says, "My object is to teach the North . . .
the awful suffering of the white man during
the dreadful Reconstruction period . . .
to demonstrate to the world that the white man must
and shall be supreme."

Dixon earlier authored *The Leopard's Spots:*
A Romance of the White Man's Burden,
dedicated to "Harriet Sweet-voiced daughter
of the old-fashioned south," published by Doubleday,
Page & Co. 1902.
To quote a couple lines re the freed negroes,
"a possible Beast to be feared and guarded." &
a line from one of the colored characters,
"Lawd hab muss on my po black soul!"

It is literary amening of "Pitchfork
Ben" Tillman.

Double-damning dastardly damsel-lusting, booze-
guzzling coons intent on domination &
race mixing.
                    A planned but never penned tome
is to be the crash & burning of Washington's
Tuskegee.

Rev'rend Dixon believes, to his soul, Lawd a' mussy,
he is the negroes' "best friend." But hear, in counter-
point, an answer to that answer: the continuing
shagging syncopation of self-proclaimed Professors
of the unofficial Order of the Nightlife
Pianoforte. Crapshooting, barhopping, freefooted,
musically erudite (often "classically
trained") knights-errant; piano pugilists' sons of
"Ethop'," the "Congo," & former slaves, with New
All African-A-merican audacious ways,
as if they're personally acquainted with
the gods, the loas, the holy ghosts, & 've
germinated & blossomed "straight from the [Dark
Continent] jungle" & Mississippian pool halls,
honky-tonks, whorehouses, & labor camps; &
Southwestern locales like Sedalia & St. Louis.

Their double consciousness melodies & African-
in-essence harmonies are blackfaced takeoffs &
turnarounds on banjoed cakewalk & minstrel ditties,
Oompha-based marches & polkas + newish
European music, bohemian, prissy-
proper & otherwise; all syncopated & such.

Irving Berlin, a.k.a. Israel Baline (18-
88–1989), Russian-born, all A-
merican pop song writer & ragtime influence,
says, "Syncopation is the soul of every true
American. Ragtime is the best heart-raiser
and worry-basher I know."
                                        Countering claims
his hit "Alexander's Ragtime Band" is stolen,
Berlin says, ". . . if a Negro could write 'Alexander,'
why couldn't I?"
                                Rumors persist, evidence builds.
Berlin's alembic version formulizes &

legitimizes the form into black music
in white face, & signals its decline as a force.

"Denial," Twain quipped, "ain't just a river in Egypt."

In the meantime, on The Great White Way, Williams &
Walker (Bert, 1874–19-
22, & George, 1873–
1911), blacks, billed as The Two Real Coons,
& Sons of Ham, star in blackface, in black partners
Marion Cook & Paul Laurence Dunbar's, colored
musical *In Dahomey*.

& Old Dan Emmett, white, famed blackened-faced minstrel
whose tune "Dixie's Land" was played at Reb Jeff Davis's
inauguration, dies.

In the meantime, Art Minstrelsy in blackface,
i.e., Cubism (claiming & renaming
the complexities of African art) is born
with Pablo Diego José Francisco
de Paula Juan Nepomuceno María
de los Remedios Cipriano de la
Santísima Trinidad Clito Ruiz y
Picasso, 1881–19-
73 European, as its daddy
when he "uses" the imagery of "savage and
mysterious" West African masks in
Les Demoiselles d'Avignon, his painted rip-off
of a 3d dimension depiction on a 2-
dimensional plane.
                    Like Berlin, Picasso denies,
denies, denies any Afric influence. My eye!

use (yooz)
v. used, us·ing, us·es

v.tr.
1. To put into service or apply for a purpose; employ.
2. To avail oneself of; practice,
3. To conduct oneself toward; treat or handle,
4. To seek or achieve an end by means of; exploit,
5. To take or consume; partake of.
n. (yoos)
1.
a. The act of using; the application or
employment of something for a purpose,
b. The condition or fact of being used,
2. The manner of using; usage.

TR thinks, "a Cubist picture, or a picture
of a misshapen nude woman, repellent
from every standpoint."

Like atoms Big Banging, forces collide. Every-
where. On all fronts.

Newton's 3d Law again.

Interacting entities exert forces on
each other. Action and Reaction are the forces,
& subjects of Newton's 3d Law of motion,
which is: If object A exerts a force
on object B, then object B exerts an
equal & opposite force on object A, or;
if A steps on B, A exerts a downward force
on B, & B, even from its lowly, put-upon
position, exerts an upward force on A.

But, there's also the problem, often whited out
by the above A regarding who is Pete &
who Repeat (i.e., innovator-imitator)
& how much it matters.

Which is which & who is who . . .
Who's on 1st?
Costello: Well then who is on first?
Abbott: Yes.
Costello: I mean the fellow's name.
Abbott: Who.
Costello: The guy on first. . . . When you pay off the first
baseman every month, who gets the money?
Abbott: Every dollar of it. . . .
(Pause)
Costello: All I'm trying to find out is what's
the guy's name on first base.
Abbott: No, what's on second base.
Costello: I'm not asking who's on second. . . .

BT, who did not come for dinner, stops, again,
by the White House to confer with TR
about his upcoming visit to Tuskegee.

Interlude
eleven

Which Treats of the Loas's Sally to Do The Work

The question is who is Pete, who Repeat? Who
gets paid every month, who gets the money,
the recognition, the glory? Questions, perhaps
for the court of last resort.

LOAS (also Lwa or L'wha) spirits, not
gods, of the Vodoun religion practiced in Haiti.
a.k.a., Mystères and the Invisibles.
Like TR's Sylphs in that regard.

Loas, akin to Christian saints or angels, act
as middle messengers between the Creator
& humans, but, rather than entities appealed to
they are served. Are individual. Specific
in their preferences, prejudices, amusements:
rhythms, songs, dances, signs, & ways of going
about their business.

If, the loas counsel, you can't join 'em, signify
& work their nerves. To beat 'em, the loas, the gods,
& the holy ghosts advise, fascinate, infect,
infiltrate.
            & as they flutter-strut like impulsive
butterflies on their migratory way, blues &
ragtimes' nectar-notes pollinate, propagate, green
the desert of negation & disregard. &
the loas, the gods, the blues Holy Ghosts, who them-
selves float like butterflies, but sting like hosts
of hornets, are pleased. These loas, gods, these Holy
Ghosts, who, when crossed or played with, come back to do some
vital butt-biting time after bluesy or

syncopated time, but who, because they are cool
& cool with it & don't go around thundering
& chest thumping, are mistaken for chumps, wimps, or
worse, but see the big picture, are counter-counter
insurgents, common consciousness invaders;
wit warriors; working in their own bluesy or
raggey way, at their own slowdrag or naggey pace,
Lawd a' mussy.
                    They ain't about flash &
skirmishes, but are about The Work. The War. They
have the patience of spirits, for that's what they are,
blue Holy Ghost spirits. & it's spirits they're concerned
with. Not flounce or short-term, but the Long Haul. In it
for all the peewees, aggies, & cat's eyes. They've got time.
The slow 4/4 footbeat, not dragslow but cadenced
as the stars, & as purposed, even if not
evident to the glancing, indifferent, or
supercilious eye, & the syncopated,
intoxicating, body-bumping, blood-thumping,
time-ragging time, & time's on their side. & these are
the same spirits, same loas, gods, & Holy Ghosts
invoked by the bad business of minstrel mockery,
blackened-faced white negro imposters doing their
hockum hocuspocus to make a buck &
batten niggers down, below the waterline &
the orlop level.

Blues booted & moving now from derisive doo-doo
to true Voodoo-Blue; practice v. white-washing
lampooning false faces masking false-hearted
Janus-jibbed hypocrites whose gate guardian god
"Looked different ways," are called to account. Moving now,
moving from mere show into The Business;
The Work.

The head man houn'gan, with ragged-timed rhythms &
chants, calls for the ancestors' loas to appear &
speak wisdom. Roused by the multimeters &
syncopation & plain-tongued, blues-based invocations,
Papa Legba parts the crossroads gates. Summoned
spirit loas, the power of Voodoo, pass through,
into the houn'gan. Thus possessed, i.e.,
inhabited & thus uninhibited,
the leader dances. Prophesies. Makes connections.
Till onlookers, their hearts' rhythm regulated
to beat as one with the houn'gan's, witness, learn, is
how the Work works. How The Business is done. See?
Lawd, Lawd a' mussy me, I say.

Iris out.
Fade in.

That fall Booker T. working his own work, counter-
coups as TR pays Tuskegee a call; sees,
in a minstrel-like show, all the coloreds, their crafts
& skills on display; praises their training
to "industrial efficiency," stays for dinner.

Iris out.
Fade in.

13

1909. An Arctic Episode in Which Is Related the Frigid Adventure of Matthew Henson When, in the Era of White Hopes, He Stands on Top of the World. & in Which Mr. Johnson Meets Mr. Burns under the Sharp Eye & Pen of Mr. London

In the meantime:
1st black band masters lead military bands. &

Matthew Henson. Man. Colored. 1866–
1955. World traveled. All requisite skills.
Is listed in expedition leader Peary's —
Robert E. (1856–1920)
crew manifest as valet. 50dollars
a month & keep. Is more. Much more. Called Kind Matthew
by the 4 Inuits, Egingwah, Ookeah,
Seegloo, & Oatah. Is brains & brawn. Tutor to
the Commander.

Is, with the Eskimos, & dogs,
who mush & tug & end as stew, first at the Pole.
Is 28 below. Henson, in kooletah,
nanookes, & kamicks, near 90° as sextant,
chronometer, & dead reckoning will amen,
stands in endless vales of vapor & white. Wind
& stars in whirring harmony overhead. With
a shiver thinks: Walked at 12, an orphan, Baltimore
to D.C. in search of . . . adventure, now am
The Negro at the North Pole, the world's top, all lines
of longitude, meet at my feet, & with earth's speed
& rotation nearly nil, time stands still.
                                        Peary,
who'd proclaimed "I *must* have fame," sickly, lame, is sledge-
hauled there, 45 minutes late. Fearing shared glory,
igs Henson's role, when, back home via their ship
the *Roosevelt,* & his story is told.
                                        Peary
retires a Rear Admiral, Hero, Henson
a Customs House clerk.

& a few new moons later:
Christmas Day. See, like a shadow on the threshold,
Jack Johnson, the "Galveston Giant," a shaved &
shone Ethiopian Samson/Goliath.
Inferior (naturally) because of race
(naturally), yet, a contender, looming at
the gate of their Golden City of the Heavyweight
division. Its king is, in the eyes of all, what
it is to be man. Mightiest of men. This Jack
has come to defy & disdain them, & challenge
their Tommy Burns, their champion & all they hold
high & holy. & they tremble day & night at their
mightiest fear that in his might this Jack (who dares
call their Tommy white as the flag of surrender!),
this black might smite their man & slay the pride of a

million with him. & yea, with a right to their
champion's jawbone the black Philistine shakes posts
& pillars & tumbles the temple down on all
who dwelt therein, making nimble & quick sport
of the lie they live & send "others" to die by.

Jack London, he who coins "Great White Hope," writes,
"The Fight!—there was no fight!"
Then more reflective says,
"Personally I was with Burns all the way.
He is a white man, and so am I. Naturally
I wanted to see the white man win."

            London, a.k.a.
John Griffith London (1876–
1916), writes rugged adventure novels
that rip & roar, *The Call of the Wild* is one.
Bastard, partially raised by an ex-slave; pseudo-
socialist son of an off-kilter suicidal
mother who channels a Native American
spirit, he swears he will never do any un-
necessary hard work. He has a character ask,
"Will the Indian, the Negro, or the Mongol
ever conquer the Teuton?" The character's answer
is, "Surely not!" He essays about whites, "Back of our
own great race adventure, back of our robberies
by sea and land, our lusts and violences and
all the evil things we have done, there is a certain
integrity, a sternness of conscience, a
melancholy responsibility of life,
a sympathy and comradeship and warm human feel,
which is ours, indubitably ours . . ."
           Odds are
Jack is a suicide at 40.

John Arthur Johnson (1878–
1946), who when the occasion calls

speaks properly, deliberately; reads, wears linen,
Tattersall & Harris Tweed, gold rings with tiger's eyes,
patent leather shoes with satin bows, collars starched
white & stiff as Jim Crow laws; apes & rapes
the idea of Western civilization;
sits, monstrous, a-squat the snow-white-gowned belly &
breast of swooning American Womanhood.

Stomachs begin to churn. Wheels begin to turn.
The U.S. of A, *the* emerging world power
powered by industrialism, capitalism,
imperialism, is in the midst of forming
& re-forming itself. It is not about
to take Jack Johnson lying down.

Johnson lives loud ("happy-go-lucky" London
profiles him), lavish, fast, "easily amused," says
London, lacks civility, in the face & mind
of white America, lacks propriety, or
decorum. Struts, brags, backs it up. Is, for all
of the above, worrisome to white *&* colored.

". . . [A]ltogether absorbed in the present moment
and therefore unmindful of the future," London
concludes, thinking he's pigeonholed Jack; types him
as typically short on brains, backbone, or will, ills
long & deep in his race, & therefore inferior,
& therefore certain to be beat up & (as the
envoy of his ilk) therefore beat down by a
superior white.

14

Of What Happens (in a Tuskegee Senior's Daydreams) When the Galveston Stevedore Meets the Tuskegee Wizard

Negro Normal School, Tuskegee, Alabama.
Panorama of building named after or paid
for by benefactors the likes of Andrew
Carnegie, Collis P. Huntington, John D.
Rockefeller, Henry Huttleston Rogers, &
Julius Rosenwald.
Class room. Education 307, 308
(History of Education—Principles of
Teaching)

Brushed, scrubbed, erect, reading. Male & female
separated by the aisle Miss Waters, class of
'05, walks. Second year back, this time as teacher
(a year of looking to end up in the Black Belt
she'd thought she could escape. That & having to let
herself be Jim Crowed—with nought backing from her
Principal—in order to spend an evening with
The Bard). She monitors over shoulders,
encouraging with a touch.

Close up. Lindsey. First
among the males to which the eye is drawn. Our focus
due not to a trick of light, or his placement
in the frame, but in or about him we see or
sense—some thing—Same bonefeeling that tips prospectors
t'ward their spot in the stream & the Eureka
sparkle in their pan of wet, shimmied sand.

Lindsey Walker, Baby Brother. Landless farmer's son
from up to Gadsden in Etowah County. Fifth
of 8; youngest boy. More truck with hoe & sack
than knack with pencil or primer, but is there
because he, as each around him, has a glint
of the gift that signals Hope, & hint of needed
grit to not quake or crack 'neath prevalent opinion,
slanted circumstance, or weight of attack.

With thought-blurred vision gazes from *her* nape
to the oaks in bud out the brightly polished panes.

Thinks:
We sit beneath the Great Emancipator's gape;
know no sweet chariot's 'bout to swing low & sweep us
on swift & safe passage by bramble, ambush, &
darksome wood, 'cross that damnable Color Line
to the far, far banks of Freedom. We know it will
be a narrow winding course over unbeaten
byways to journey's end. The Race, it's said, will be led
by the Upper Tenth—which thinks, we Tuskegeeites
mere draft mules to their thoroughbreds.

Thinks:
President Booker T. (who praises Slavery
for its introduction of coloreds to Jesus
& the Work Ethic) believes we at the bottom
(Tuskegee graduates & below) play our part

learning 3 Rs, & his founding philosophy:
Persistence, Patient Subordination, & Spade
Husbandry. In a world where Jack Johnson dresses
'em off & knocks 'em down till they can't get up
no more, the Master Manipulator trains us
not to compete, but to comply. Just smart enough
to, without being burdens, accept our second class
place.

Remembers:
bunting-draped stands with invited Presidents,
Industries' Captains, legislative bigwigs, &
select coloreds & whites of lofty rank, & we,
the student body, to impress with our Progress
& Discipline, carrying school-grown sugar cane
& cotton bolls, pass in review, orderly,
in step, like stock for sale.

Remembers:
William Howard Taft & Andrew Carnegie
were 2 who paid Tuskegee a call: Taft (18-
57–1930), ton-sized future
President (27th), & stumpy Andrew
Carnegie (1835–1919),
with no more schooling than a cat, but is the 2d
richest man in all the world.

Remembers:
the different faces Washington dons for each,
a different show, a different speech. Jack Johnson
shows the same at every turn. Bad. Black. Calls them by
their name. What face would we take to take on the world
if this Institution were Dandy Jack Johnson's—
What face would our Principal wear if Champion Jack
came?—not that he'd be invited, not that he'd accept.

Ah, but if Jack, the Galveston Stevedore, were to come:
Come arage. The 8 horses of his REO
Model G Roadster pounding like dark jungle drums
& cutting a reckless rut 'neath a cloud of
chicken-scattering dust. At rest it purrs & pants
like a pre-pounce killer-cat. Its canary-yellow
matching Jack's duster, gloves, & cap.
                                (Would he dare
a white woman with him? Cozy'd in wicked ermine,
gaudy plumes, & diamond rings?)
                          Jack'd strut to his
lettered host, golden grin agleam, put the
emphasis on Doctor, *as he pumped his arm.*

Principal Washington, who missed nothing, would note
our attention paid the pugilist. He'd think we'd
only think Jack excess. Reckless success.
A knothole peep to greener pastures. He'd think
his teaching Prudence would be set back many years.

Whatever the final decision the opening
rounds would be the Champ's.

Asked about the Black Leonardo, Professor
Carver, our second main attraction; apologies
to Jack for his absence; sudden illness being
the excuse. In truth, Carver—(who when young survived
by the domestic arts)—feeble as a teacher,
muttering doddering doggerel only he could
understand—would, in self-defense against the force
of Jack's Black Barbarian repute, declare
a slight lightness in his head, seek refuge in his room
at the top of the stairs, where, to calm his nerves would,
with fingers twisted as twigs, knit socks or mittens
& sip cleansing tea brewed from peanuts & roots.

Little does Washington know, we know brash but
cagy Jack; see him plain— In the ring he is cool
as an iceman's wagon, rational as a judge.
It is there when & where he confounds them with his
brainy, managed mayhem; letting them try to harm him,
then taunts, &, calculating as an auditor,
drubs their rash attempt, until, face-first, they fall.

Yes, we know what BT knows not, or
in the harness of his politics has forgot,
or opts to withhold, as too bold for fit in his
meek beliefs.

We know, as Jack must, whites are not fighting him, nor
even with his defeat will they beat him, will only
have found a new way to dupe themselves from
fully knowing, as he, & we know them.

Jack is their dark refraction seen fully face to
face. Is their sought payment in the same coin for
the greed & wreck of their wild reach.
                              You know what I
want—Jack taunts them—*my damned due! The prize, & means to*
its end, I learned from you.
                              He is the unlunking core
of their cold furor to have, hold, & hate, that must,
with whips, rods, & switches of self-retribution,
be flogged into whimpering submission before
the twisted inflictions of their Anglo-Saxon
nature can be forgiven.
                        "Well, no pain, no gain,"
Jack reckons in his willing fulfillment
of their need. & in payback for their crimes & slights
against him & his, enters the ring of mirrors,
where round after round, pounds the flesh of hulking
combatants, preforced by the great white hope of their

willful conviction. & plodding in their mulish zeal,
tilt & flail as he ducks their thrusts, calls them Boss,
& counters with syncopated thunderbolts,
inquiring, with piteous concern, while they
stumble & totter like pole-axed cows, *if they've had
enough.*

Yes, it is there when & where, every time they
wheel about he does just so, every time they reel
about he thumps their old Jim Crow. Yes, Great White Hopes
who come, so full of pride & fight, wheel & reel about
then fall face-first before Jack Johnson's righteous might.

If, in a stolen moment, I, Lindsey, the day-
dreamer, soon to face the world, could ask Jack Johnson,
Notorious Heavyweight Champion, how,
as entangled, near or far, with them as we are, how
to keep up my defense, yet attack, while paddling
backward, tapping them upside their heads at will; ask
him too, how to support a lady, albeit
colored, one like sweet Louisa, one row up &
across the aisle—Louisa—swan-necked Louisa,
quality, but spur-of-the-moment Louisa,
Louisa, smart as a tack Louisa. Turns his
tongue thick as cold sorghum.
                              At the tap & screech
of their teacher chalking, tomorrow's assignment
on the slate, with flourished cursive slants & loops,
calling his attention from the window in time
to see *Her* half smile as she returns to her reading
from her glance back at him.

Ask rash & crashing Jack how to be prudent
& patient, yet oak-hearted enough to wow &
win a wonder such as *her*—Louisa, swan-necked,
quality, but spur-of-the-moment Louisa,

Louisa, smart as a tack Louisa. How to be
a man worthy of her within the brutish time's
confines, where, for whites to want is to have, while we
stand outside, our hands on the gate, our heads bowed.

1909-1910. Treats of the Blues, Black Movies, & NAACP Coming into Focus as Whitefolks Act Ugly, Puff, Pow

This as Niagarites, like a barrel of crabs,
plummet over the falls of infighting, crash
on the rocks of ego sniping, dissolve to mist,
evaporate in a cloud of frustration,
& rain down on the nascent soil of the
National Association for the Advancement
of Colored People—seeded & overseen
by white, social, & Socialists' concerned cash.
Du Bois is recruited as Director
of Publicity & Research. Putting academe
behind him he accepts & quickly walks away . . .

Puff.
Pow.

Many 1000s go(ne).

In the meantime,
Rodin, Kandinsky, Mackintosh, Kokoschka,

Mahler, & Gide are busy over there.

In the meantime,
over here Negro male life expectancy is
34 as attention is refocused &
redoubled on keeping negroes in their place, but,
like buoys on a sea of ingenuity,
a couple forward-thinking colored boys surface,
bound, & bob about among the white caps:

down on the Mississippi there's W. C.
Handy; out West is Oscar Micheaux.
                                    Handy,
William Christopher (18-
73–1958), out of Memphis
& many minstrel bands.
                        Micheaux (1884–
1951), 5th of 13 children,
grandson of former slaves, former farmer, coal miner,
& Pullman porter, b. in Metropolis,
Illinois, with a fusion philosophy
= parts BT & Horace Greeley (18-
11–1872), Micheaux,
a born self-promoter, with more penny-pinching
chutzpa than talent, & no more farming savvy
than authorial or film-making skill, homesteads
on South Dakota acreage, pens mythbusting,
darkskinned-can-do preachment novels; publishes &
hawks them door to door; makes movies of them; loses
the farm (to a scheming father-in-law as he
tells it); becomes Father of Race films.

Handy has slow, but less racially tainted or
tinny ears than his white counterparts. Formally
trained, with "composer" & "arranger" titles
of that rank of cultural commerce to prove it;

his hearing, honed on the grindstone of Jim Crow tenets
& minstrel-circuit backroads, & tutored in the
hard-&-fast-name-it-&-claim-it business tradition
of white "discoverers," becomes, like them, Daddy
of an existing entity. Thinks the creature
monotonous & coarse in its low relations.
Bewails the raucous reactions it educes.
But, by mere putting pen to paper, transcribing,
he, by conjecture lays claim on its concoction
& soul. He tones down its black, its raw, straightens out
some twists & wangs—misdirects its reason with grafts
& lesions, proves with the resulting interlards,
zambos, gallimaufry, & salmagundi, the re-
verse of their miscegenation spiel. Imposes
a form, changes a story. Thereby lays Handy's
path to fame & glory.

In the meantime, the lucky of the down-home,
black-bottom folk, tipping away from the hellish
ways that form the blues core,
                        Puff.
                        Pow.
                        Many 1000s go(ne)
                                    cross that up North shore
where they might can walk along, side by side, if not
hand in hand, with their desires, moaned & sung &
shouted about in their blues, which until then, from
back before anybody can say, took as many
forms as were necessary to get its
necessary Work done.

Hear the oompa oompa oompa oompa
as the rich get richer, the poor need more, time &
the Press & Church & State & the A-merican
populace consumers, the Americanists,
Forward March, as the band plays on.

See:
RACE RIOT. Springfield, Illinois, City of
Honest Abe's interment. Much plying
of the torch in colored quarters. Many blacks beaten.
2 blacks killed.
     Fearing invasive full-force, bare-faced,
plain as charred wood & violated black flesh Jim Crow
Lynch Law solutions, the question can no longer
be begged. No longer able to pretend the Race
Problem simply Dixie's dilemma, Northern whites'
liberal spirit is incinerated.

The N. A. A. C. P. steps up.

16

In Which Is Related the Unfortunate Adventure That Befalls Mr. Jeffries When He Encounters 2-Fisted Mr. Johnson . . . & Other Unlooked-for Happenings

1910

to America of the 4th of July, as
viewed by the colored 2d class, Frederick Douglass
said 58 years prior: "your celebration
is a sham; your boasted liberty, an unholy
license; your national greatness, swelling vanity; . . .
are empty and heartless; your denunciation
of tyrants, brass-fronted impudence; your shouts
of liberty and equality, hollow
mockery; your prayers and hymns . . . a thin veil
to cover up crimes which would disgrace
a nation of savages."

Independence Day. Reno, Nevada. Former
Heavyweight Champion, Jim (James J.) Jeffries,
now alfalfa farmer, is recruited as the

"Great White (& last ditch) Hope" to recapture
The Title from black Jack Johnson & redraw the
Color Line.
    Keeping it *mano a mano*, Johnson says,
"I honestly believe that in pugilism I am
Jeffries' master." First class signifying or low
class, racially insensitive choice of words?
The Press does what the Press does: goes nuts.
"Johnson believes he's Jeff's master," print pundits
editorialize, formal with the former,
familiar with the latter, while stirring boiling
bile in the racist pot.
      ". . . and it is my purpose,"
Jack, who drives fast, consorts with & marries white women,
continues, as if he is not out on a limb
& in it up to his neck, "to demonstrate this
[this ass whupping he's predicting] in the most
decisive way possible . . ."
      "It's the money
I'm after, man," Jeffries insists.

Jack London, racial schizoid, nudges Jeffries forward
toward his bruising, saying "Jeff, it's up to you.
The White Man must be rescued."

Shotguns are oiled, ammo loaded. Ropes noosed, Jim Crow
& hellhounds readied to be loosed. "Let me say
in conclusion," Jack says over ½ way to his
close, "that I believe the meeting between Mr.
Jeffries and myself will be a great test of strength,
skill, and endurance." Then, in the tradition of
trickster masters, shifts gears on 'em, having covered
the human, he rags over into the cultural.
"The tap of that gong will be music to me." *BOING!*
That does it. It's etched in stone, time to be about it.
It is Jeffries's duty, to God, country, &

the notion of Anglo-Saxon pre-eminence
to re-right Holy Writ re their rite, in matters
of might to (as the last left standing) write the last word.

Contradicting his earlier assertion Jim says,
"I am going into this fight for the sole purpose
of proving that a white man is better than a
Negro."
        The remark pulses with the proper
supremacist *sturm & drang*, huh? Reckon that means
any white man & *any* Negro.
                          Cue
"Ride of the Valkyries."
                          "All Coons Look Alike to Me"
is struck up by the ringside band instead.

The Wizard, who in some other context says,
"Character is power," & "Excellence is to
do a common thing in an uncommon way,"
has round by round fight reports telegraphed
to Tuskegee's Assembly Hall for them all to cheer.

Jim refuses the pre-match handshake. Nothing to do,
as they say, but to do it. Once more unto the breach,
dear friends, once more.

Tap.
Gong.
Puff.
Pow.
& *the righteous warfare* is on. Jim, intent on
abolishing so errant a strain from contention,
assumes the offensive. Countering Jim's assault
& his backer's savage songs (that as the contest
continues, turn to ones of Sorrow), Jack, string bassist
in his leisure, begins with a steady, bluesy,

barrelhouse doom-doom-doom-doom, to show them the things
that will happen soon, then, as Jim jousts, lunges, &
tilts with whirling flurries like a longnailed Great Dane
on a sheet of Antarctica ice, Jack, carefree
as a boy, fiddles with Jim, shifting rhythms
in jabbing & tapping, teasing & taunting, tattooing,
saying, over the noise & uproar, *"Here! Here! Big Jim,*
Now is the time to show the strength of your mighty arms."

Tap, gong to Jeffries's jaw & head. Johnson knocks
The Hope down.
Puff.
Pow.

& for Jeffries (& all the throng transfixed) it is
chapter 1 of a Revelation. Hearing the words
of Jack's prophecy & the time is at hand.
& they see who was, & who is, & who is to come.
& each eye, clear or dazed, is a faithful witness,
that he is more man, of that mode, than any they
can contrive. & they know, with woeful regret, that
it will be written, & it will be filmed, & that word,
blaring like a trumpet, will go out to New York,
Philadelphia, Detroit, St. Louis, Cleveland,
& to Chicago where Negroes swelling with pride,
in multitudinous numbers reside.

Jack, strategically shifting rhythms at will,
from slow, blistering-as-Joshua's-blue-flame-dog-
day-hot-sun that stood still in the middle of the sky
& did not hasten to set!; to jerky-jagged
as a Jack Rabbit outjuking a beagle through
the briar, doubling back, circling &
beelining for its burrow all at once;
to midtempo, like a smoking locomotive
chugging, with death's determination from

the vanishing point on down the line;
jabbing in hummingbird flurries & stumpthumping,
staccato, sledgehammer rights; all with the ease
of bleached linens breeze-drying on a May Monday morn.

& his head, this lawless giant's, is shining marble,
& his body an oak trunk, black & annealed as if
furnace-fired, his teeth are ingots of gold,
& his words, as if raining from the clouds like spears,
jab & stab, saying: *Fear not, I am the first*
but not the last. I am nothing but behold
I am forevermore. I will sport the crown,
& hold the key to the highway. Let your scribes write
& your cameras record that, yes, there is a
spirit guiding my left hand, & a mystery
guiding my right hand, & that it fetched the stars dancing,
like enchanted, windmilling madness in your head,
& in your eyes as you fall at my feet like a
dead man.
Amen.

. . .*"2!"*;
& for Jim, light collapses & time & history
are simultaneous contraction-expansions,
& are out of joint;

. . .*"3!"*;
                          uncoils like a waking snake; or
ribbon in unspooling twisting curl;

. . .*"4!"*;
pastpresentfuture—meet mesh meld, in the shadowy
infinite; coalesce, a harmony
of contradictions stretched to their elastic limit . . .
Where—was I—& who? Jim, waking, thinks. Why
is the light so bright, & what is that noise?;

. . . "*5!*";
& as his head clears, Jim Jeffries (1875–
1953), "The Boilermaker," bullstrong,
quick as a lie, bloodletter, rib-breaking 1-punch
knockouter, takes punishment like a Georgia mule,
sees, through the blear, Jack standing ape-arrogantly
over him, fist cocked, sun gleaming off his black &
bald as a bad luck 8-ball head.

In this instant interchange of their eye-lock, time,
at its limit, leaps ahead, reverses, snaps back
realigned: 1st-last, back to front; passed past pretense.
Sham, lies, glossed portrayals shatter; reassemble
as raw reality, recognized by the amassed
(aghast!) for what it is, & forever has been,
& its folly never again can as fully be.

"*6!*"
Johnson grins his golden grin, mocks his Caucasian
combatant bruised to a pulp, dares him to rise.

"*&7!*"
The assembled on their feet, fear & flop sweat
blacking the bands, armpits, & collars of their
skimmers & shirts, hear him, see this as more than
monkey shines, or sanctioned legalized assault, &
are sore afraid.

Jeffries, at the crowd's despairing exhortations,
& with the weight of the Western World on his brawny
but battered shoulders, is weak, but manages,
with Herculean effort, to heave up,
(Puff.)
        till,
The Force of Darkness strikes again. Heaven falls.
(Pow!)

&!

down! goes! White Supremacy! Knocked out of the ring!
Shock & awe. Jeffries's seconds push him to his
feet & back into the ring. The White Hope, to quote
B.B. King, "getting some outside help he didn't
really need," is punched, pounded, & knocked from the ring
again . . . & . . .

It's over . . . All over . . .

"White Man Outclassed

by His

Opponent from the First

Tap [rat-tat-tap]

of the Gong"

John Arthur Jack Johnson, having stood against all
comers,

WINS

IN 15 ROUNDS, is

Still

The

Un-

Disputed

Black

Heavyweight Champion

of the World!

"I Couldn't Come Back," says
Former Champion, Helpless
After Third Knockdown.

It is natural to the breed, groused some in dim
barroom post-mortems, their derbies tipped back,
counterbalance to their tilt-forward tendency

under the weight of the rye. Jungle tutoring
carried over, they conclude. Or, stogie-chomping
beer-sippers muse, t'was some Dark Continent deity,
or demon more likely, guided the coon. Either way,
be Goren, the jig is up, our man down.

In sight of the loss

RIOTS COUNTRY WIDE

the race affects frowns,

MANY COLORED INJURED

pretend they haven't heard,

8 DIE

but away from the watchful eye, they buck, do breaks,
& cut Cakewalking capers.
                              Deemed too hot for
public viewing, film of the calamity is,
by Congress, banned, border-to-border, coast-to-coast.
But, they despair, there's no way to put the clamps on
the outcome. The direct indirect effect will,
at lickety-split speed, leap, with that voodoo they do,
space & time. Jigs are likely, even now, rumbling
& jumping from Kansas to the Congo from the
foundation-shaking pummeling put on our poor Jim
by him who crowned himself a man, a claim, shown up
as we are, none can now deny.

Hangdog & smarting it is time to switch venues,
time to change the rules.

The report of his April 21, 19-
10 death, this time no exaggeration, Mark Twain,
Samuel Langhorne Clemens, "Known to Everyone—
Liked by All," is paid a visit by Mister Death,
The Impartial Friend, "the only immortal
who treats us all alike . . . the soiled and the pure,

the rich and the poor, the loved and the unloved,"
missed the brouhaha, the uproar, rumpus,
the continued to-do of the great white hope
to ground the manhood out of Jack, & all who knew
him for what he was.

Fade out.

1912-1914. In Which Woodrow Wilson, Jack Johnson, & James Reese Europe Figure . . . & Other Unsought Happenings

Iris in:

as, in the meantime
they come to order as the up beat down beat strikes up
the band, & the rich get richer, the poor need more,
2, THREE, 4 & Time & the Press & Church & State
& the American populace consumers,
the Americanists Forward March, as the band
plays on.

& as the moon of hope wanes, dog gone their hard-luck souls,
if the sun of backlash don't also rise: prospects
of progress ain't just wan, but in retreat. The heat
of Jim Crow's reckoning causes popular taste
for things colored to cool, & COON STOCK DROPS
like the dewaxed wings of Daedalus's kid:

Spite cited as cause of this nose-lopping recoil.

Huddled muddle are cut off from their primal source
of cultural inspiration. (Fever follows chill,
& after a short cycle of dis-order,
recovery, & relapse, the patients revive
as they hear.)

Close up:
James Reese Europe (1881–1919),
colored, composer, community organizer,
conductor of "the premiere African-American
musical organization in the country."
100+ strong & taking his cue from Handy's
homogenized version of the blues they play light-
weight classics, waltzes, Sousaesque struts &
refined Rags; nothing too ragged. Respectable
enough to look as if they won't stink up, tear down,
or sully the sanctity of a joint. They
quietly integrate Carnegie Hall.

Cut to:
Long shot:
When Astors & Vanderbilts dance to Europe &
his Clef Club's Exclusive Society
Orchestra's tunes, Colored dance enters the ballroom
seductively as a hint of scent in madam's
cleavage.

Iris in.

See:
1913. Thomas Woodrow Wilson (18-
56–1924), left eye high-blood
pressure blind for a time. Top hat, frock coat, *pez nez*.
Precise & postured as a rail, runs against big
business's President William Howard Taft,
Socialist Eugene V. Debs, & reformer TR.

Gets but 41% of the pop vote, but
is 28th President after the
Electoral College turns the trick.

Says, "America lives in the heart of every man
everywhere who wishes to find a region where
he will be free to work out his destiny as
he chooses." Wilson believes in predestination.
"God ordained that I should be the next President,"
he declares. He has, just in case, Du Bois's
endorsement, & vote. "I am," Wilson admits,
"a vague, conjectural personality, more
made up of opinions & academic pre-
possessions than of human traits & red corpuscles."
Or, he fails to include, racial compassion.
The band plays on.

As will Lillian Gish in *Birth of a Nation,*
& Stepin Fetchit in *Judge Priest,* J(ohn). Edgar Hoover,
proudly does major domo duty as senior
captain of his high school ROTC marching along
Pennsylvania Avenue at Wilson's
inaugural inaugural. *2, 3, 4.*

Tuskegee Normal and Industrial
Institute. Tuskegee, Alabama.
Principal Booker Taliaferro
Washington. Educator, country gentleman
every inch. Poses. Picture of patience & self-
control. Fedora, cravat, 3-piece suit, & gaiters
or greaves, leather, shiny black Statue still, astride
his gelding. As if bronzed in black & white, as in
distant D.C. the parade passes him by. *2-3-4.*

Hoover, a year later, is a government clerk.

Hum hm h*mummm*
2-3
Hum hm huum***mummm***

Iris out.
Fade in.

Jack Johnson, pardoned for his athleticism,
(natural to negroes as whiskers on felines),
but not for the arrogant funk he sprays like a
Tomcat, nor the liberties he thinks go with it,
like marrying into the "other world." &, ah,
though the wheels of justice grind slowly, grind they do.
"Our greatest weakness lies in giving up," the U.S.
reasons, as Edison has it in his quote.
"The most certain way to succeed is always to
try just one more time."
                              For acting like a man,
Johnson, the 1st ever (on their 2d try) is
convicted for trumped-up Mann Act violation,
interstate rail transport of a woman for
purposes of prostitution & debauchery,
a.k.a. the White Slave Act (wink & nod). It is
in absentia, since Jack, seeing the cursive
on the writ, gets his hat & exiles himself
& his golden grin from the U.S.'s purple
mountains, alabaster cities, & fruited plains
for greener European pastures where his
acting in relations "with people of other
races as if prejudice did not exist" played
to a bigger audience.

"Just because something doesn't do what you planned it
to do doesn't mean it's useless." "There is always,"
Edison says, echoing America's anti-
Johnson attitude, "a better way."

The federal judge, with his ruling, warning all black
men off white women, amens Edison.

BT says he does not defend or condemn Jack.
But calls that of which Jack is accused evil. Scolds
that the individual Negro is as
capable of doing harm & bringing shame
to the race as whites combined. Rests his case.

An other Johnson, James P. (1894–
1955), colored pianist &
composer, calling on the spirit of Jack Johnson,
no direct blood relation, conjures the
Carolina Shout. It is rough & rural, strides
loose & bluesy, reminds of boll weevils, Jim Crow,
hot Dixie nights, floods, lynchings, the Galveston Giant's
k.o.s. Is uplifting. Moves the black peasantry like
Norfolk and Western hopper cars move cargos
of coal, & they hear it & Hop like bull frogs, Lope
like buzzards, Trot like turkeys, Scratch like barnyard hens
ragging till the break of dawn.

James Reese, feeding downtown's desire to slum
uptown, concocts a dance comingling ragtime's
One Step with the Turkey Trot & the march.
Gets the Castles, Vernon (1881–
1918) & Irene (1893–
1969), a white dancing couple, who
earlier hitched on his bandwagon, to front for him.
Acknowledging their debt to dances long done by
"Your colored people," they scrape off just enough black
& blue of its spontaneous nature to gussie
it up in the cosmetic veneer fit in
ballrooms of chic. The Castles & the dance sweep
country & Continent.

18

1913-1914. In Which the Smart Money Was Still Not in Coon Futures . . . William Monroe Trotter Confronts Woodrow Wilson, & Other Unpleasant Matters That Deserve to Be Recorded

The President's chair barely warm Woodrow Wilson
convenes a covert meeting, plots the segregation
of Black federal civil servants, restrooms, &
restaurants, of Railway Mail, Post Offices,
Navy & Treasury Departments, Bureau
of Engraving and Printing. No more black faces
in those places. "I sincerely believe it to be
in their interest," Wilson says. Because, he says
to Trotter in a White House meeting, "segregation
was caused by friction between the colored and white clerks,
and not done to injure or humiliate
the colored clerks, but to avoid friction."
                                           Trotter,
incensed (still), stands eyes locked with Wilson, & in word
& tone froth with insolent indignation, calls

the Presbyterian preacher's boy to account,
cross-questions his racist, back-turning jump down &
spin around on colored human rights, & gets put out;
told by Wilson, who'd never "been addressed in such
an insulting manner" never to darken
the White House door again.
        &, yet again,
Du Bois, over-slow on the uptake, but quick
on the back track, tilts, again t'ward Trotter's side, says,
Wilson is "by birth . . . unfitted for largesse of view
or depth of feeling about racial injustice."

Of D. W. Griffith

1915.
50th year after the War's end.
Floods, sad soil, & boll weevils further deplete
the South of its crops &

D. W.
(David Llewelyn Wark) Griffith.
(1875–1948.)
Director. Producer. Screen writer. Actor.
Son of heroic Confederate army Colonel.

Master shot reveals the very model of the
modern movie maker: wide-brimmed Stetson, shirt of
gabardine, jodhpurs, boots, & for good measure
the appropriate prop, a riding crop. Dolly
in slowly to reveal close up:

features obscured by darkness. Hooded gaze focused.
Sharp. Hooked beak he hates but uses to underpin
impression of Imperial demeanor. But
until the deed is done his days will be a shadow.

Light will be darkness, & darkness light.

                                               Flashback:
is little David who in morning light sees the
shimmering face of Jesus. & face to face says,
"My name is David, and you know what that means &
always has." Is David Llewelyn who says in
his heart & unto himself, Yes. & hides his face of fear
& shyness. Hides his face of unease with women
& with men. Hides his face of shame for not having.
Hides the face of his salacious savors for hordes
of "light women" & nervous little sister-like
pet nymphets ripe as Eden's forbidden fruit. &
hides the face of the bitter testament of his
humbled braggadocio daddy, Thunder Jake.
Hides them behind the mask of Actor. Hides them
behind the mask of Screen Writer. Hides them behind
the masks of film Director & Producer &
Son of Rebel Army Colonel who never
escaped the war, who remains distant, who squanders
what remains, before leaving wife & 7
beloved children behind. Yes. A shadow, wider
& deeper-dark than that beneath the brim of that hat,
is the thrall cast by the pall of his K.K.K.-
affiliated Daddy. Jake. Who bears proudly
'till death did them part, Kentucky Colonel-hood &
the red badge won during his gallant defense
of his by-God Given Right to own slaves. Dies, his
big daddy does, in little David Llewelyn's
10th year. The boy blames blacks, he does. Is niggers he
figures. The Cause is 'cause of the cussed coloreds,
& of course when Thunder Jake rides war-ward, Uncle
Henry, his faithful black lackey, is in tow. Jake
swears by Henry. Sets store by him. While the shy boy
is left behind with Mother, dour, stern as stone,
& a nest of doting, sprite-like sisters. Oh, the
niggers, is the damnable niggers, *their* black fault,

laments the bereaved Griffiths upon their scion's
demise. If the niggers, the damnable niggers
only labored like they should, the family
Griffith would not have been cast down into privation.
Oh, the niggers, is the damnable niggers causes
contempt to be rained down on Dixie's noble off-
spring; shame to be brought on the face of the South & all
mighty men & angelic maidens who love her.
& the Klan is the answer, the path back
to dignity & resurrection of the Southern
White men to their place of Natural Mastery.
Is David Llewellyn who, in his heart, vows, some-
day he'll tell the world of the true tale of the South's
reasons. & until that deed is devised & done
his days will be a shadow, light would be darkness,
& darkness light. Yes.

Which Treats, circa 1911, of Trust & Fulfillment, & the First Sally That Booker T. Takes to View the Ingenious Work of D.W.

TRUST
noun
1. Assured resting of the mind on the integrity, veracity, justice, friendship, or other sound principle, of another person; confidence; reliance. 2. Credit given; especially, delivery of property or merchandise in reliance upon future payment; exchange without immediate receipt of an equivalent; as, to sell or buy goods on trust.

FULFILLED
adj : completed to perfection.

Early riser. BT with time on his hands before the appointment to sell his story, put on his show for the gentleman of affairs.

Sunshine plastered on shiny windows, & weathered
walls with shouts of billboards & loud-lettered handbills
competing for notice amid auto horns, hooves'-
clacks, & trolley-clangs. His apologies as he
zigzags, hat-doffed against the bustle: hard-eyed, clean-
shaven, & mustached in derbies & boaters, &
knickered delivery boys, & big-apple-capped
shoeshiners, & newsies hawking the morning's most
current events. & the tide of giggles &
jabbering woodpecker conversations of powdered
secretaries & shop-girls in cartwheel-sized hats,
shirtwaist tops, bloused skirts hobbled at midshin, ending
at bared ankles, forcing minced, hard-heeled steps rata-
tating like jerky, rapidly tapping ragged-
timed typewriter keys. & command of brass-buttoned
& star-badged policemen in bobby-helmets, &
clinched-mouthed caution of silent city negroes.

Frivolity & idleness rankle BT's
core, but down a side street he slues, & hat brim low
into a nickelodeon he ducks. Its placard
promises 2 1-reelers,

HIS TRUST

&

HIS TRUST FULFILLED

by D. W.
Griffith. Said to be mastering for the masses
a new means of amusement. Why not a morning
reprieve before his meeting with the robber-baron-
humanitarian in the site from which said
captain set his course?

Pointed, without protest, to his assigned section,
sits. In the dark. Anonymous. Taps his toe
against the waiting, wanting to rein in the reel
& flicker of his thoughts, day & night bounding beyond
his will, like newly foaled fillies:

                          a lynching per week
at least;

        in the coming election Wilson, TR, & Taft likely
candidates with little fault to find;

                        unmindful of the
privilege of a Tuskegee teachership
ungrateful faculty whining & sniping
at his authority like Du Bois & the Wells
woman.

The photo-play begins:

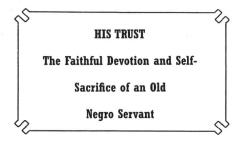

HIS TRUST

The Faithful Devotion and Self-

Sacrifice of an Old

Negro Servant

White actors as blacks; minstrelsy moved forward
in this newest form—but used to that: remembers
coalblackened-faced whites in the mine at Malden,
with their already raw, low-side manner, so begrimed
no difference can be told till after Saturday night's
tin tub scrubbing.

Civil War South. Master/Husband, sword at his waist,
leaving wife & child to join the glorious Gray.
Slave George, uncle-aged, good, sober, trusty, always
but a step away, vows to look after Missus,
Missy, & all.

Battle rages, the Colonel falls.
Little Miss rides George horsey back as sad word &
sword arrives. Missus wavers but stays staunch with George's
support, even when vile Yankees loot & torch
the homestead—with Missy inside! Takes 2 trips
but faithful George saves child & sword. Then provides his
homeless charges rough shelter, & sleeps dog-loyal
(companion, sentry, protection) outside across
his hovel's threshold.

Iris out.
The End.

Then:

```
HIS TRUST FULFILLED
```

After the war, yet still under manumitted
George's wing, Mother/Widow, passing beloved sword
to him, passes. He, secretly deeds "his savings"
to daughter for college, & leaves her with good white
family. In the dark she thanks the whiteman
for her good fortune & weds her English cousin.
George in tatters & tempted, thinks thievery, but
doesn't, yet is exiled still. But his trust fulfilled,
sits at home, selfless, with the symbolic sword.

Iris out.
The End.

So struck near dumb is BT as the stories rise
before & in him—like Sunday morning sun back
at his first bright, unhaunted childhood moments
in the home of Mrs. Viola Ruffner—that
only after the action stops & the lights rise
realizes there's been a piano player
all along; like a ghostly, knowing guide clueing,
accompanying, cuing to feelings, thoughts.

Urge to leap up, sing out at what he's just seen,
like besotted sinner coming to sweet Je-sus;
rail against the coalface mountain of silence of
(in)difference from the others in attendance,
rising, gathering to shuffle, unconverted, out.

Hope! He wants to run to block the Exit & shout.
The reward of Loyalty & Trust. This,
Hallelujah, is it! Hope! The rock on which to build
our new prayer house, don't you see!

Thinks: This Griffith, a Southerner loves the South
& its many parts as much as I!

We in our secret, oft'-denied humanity;
in our separate darkness, separated
but singular in need; in our 1 blind blood; 1
throbbing blind heart; 2 teary blind eyes, grope toward
each other's answer of bonds of Trust
& affection &, oh yes, Loyalty, through the
woeful, intolerable gape between us.

Thinks (as he doesn't often) of art: Perhaps (with
this new form—Southern. American. More than fancies
of kings, knights, & swords) is Art with reason for it.
& it does have its place. Is a new bag of tricks
& way of showing our (mine & this Griffith's) love
of what we love, then, now, & to be.

Is Art more moving than Church. Is dug from a deeper
vein, a richer lode, running back the length of my life,
of my being, to the quivering pap of the
formation of my soul & heart. The me I am.

The gape of Fear, my brothers, BT wants to shout. *Fear,*
Hope's opposite, that tells us it is better to—

slay that blind yearning for kindness & trust that
cowers in us; better to kill that truth than let it
free, be exposed to the wild of slights & serpents.
Better to kill it, Fear whispers within the dark,
dank & dripping chambers of our own cold-walled hearts;
better to cuddle & coo to it as we pinch
its nose, seal its mouth, & steel our muscles against
its kicks & thrashes till its fierce argument
for release is spent, & its pulse has pounded its
last, & then, & only then is our yearning
against Hope! safe—ours. Yes—but no, brothers. That is
in dutiful service only to our basest fear
of the consequences of our knowledge, & of
the danger of ourselves exposed.

Thinks:
The power of this form, this storytelling &
play-acting (albeit in blackface & without
words!) burrows & blasts away all impediments
to the source. Shows as clearly & cleanly & simply
as one's first glimpse then gawk at his own reflection
in a spring pond. The recognition. Shock. Wonder.
Joy & shame. & birth of Hope, & knowledge of all
that needs be known: door from dark to light; first wail
to last whimper; cradle to cooling board. Hope!
Sole & lonesome answer against all else. Hope! Hope!

I will permit no fear to narrow and degrade
my soul by making me obey it; stumble down
no path that circles back into its own damn'd
inception. No.

Thinks:
Trust & fulfillment in the unequal(ed) unit
of donor & donee, tutor & taught, to do,
as George did, what is right! & as, when I was

in her employ, Mrs. Viola Ruffner to me,
a raw & dirty, densely ignorant urchin:
even after I'd run away then driven back
by my failures she took me in, instilling
Discipline, Cleanliness, Order, entrusting with
Responsibility, rewarding Honesty,
showing Gratitude, to me! & me back to her.
The deed. Needed & done. 1 2-faced coin.

Yes. The way up to the out of the dark
is along the track of kindness, trust, & caring.
If we but let kindness & trust work their wiles
against all contrivances, we will find forgiveness
for our sins, each & everyone, however conceived
or committed.
                    But BT shouts none of it.
Gathers himself instead. With little more than an
hour lost, goes, blinking in sunlight & the world
as it is.

Bee-lines now with unapologetic stride. Man
in motion. About his business. Star in his own
photo-play. With mathematic or musical logic
his likeness, in smoothly skimming panorama,
repeats, repeats, humming frame-by-shop-front-pane-frame.
Merged, in that chammied 1-dimension, with the street's
mirrored commerce & clot: sandwich-board strollers &
street-hucksters' handouts: samples, pamphlets promising—
with exchange of cash from hand to hand—more, newer;
quicker; safer; longer lasting; twice as sweet.

Of Potential, Energy, Counterweight, Counterbalance, Elevator, & Booker T. Going Up the Shaft & Down Again

POTENTIAL
1: existing in possibility: capable
of development into actuality.
2: expressing possibility; *specifically:*
of, relating to, or constituting a verb phrase
expressing possibility, liberty, or
power by the use of an auxiliary with
the infinitive of the verb (as in "he may give").

ENERGY
The capacity to do work or produce change.

POTENTIAL ENERGY: $PE = mgh$
capacity for doing work that a body
possesses because of its position or
condition.

COUNTERWEIGHT
an equivalent weight or force.

COUNTERBALANCE
1: a weight that balances another
2: a force or influence that offsets or checks
an opposing force.

Arrives early. Questioned hard by the lobby guard.
Plip. Sent out, around, back to the banged & splintered-
walled freight-hauler—

ELEVATOR
One who, or that which, raises, lifts, or exalts; as
a mechanical contrivance.

Teeth clinched.

Plip.

Breath held.

BT, to calm himself within its cagey confines,
repeats:
There is the shaft.
There is a motor
That is in the shaft.
There is a pulley
Hitched to the motor
That is in the shaft.
There is a rope
Looped over the pulley
Hitched to the motor
That is in the shaft . . .

Plop.

Eyes squeezed shut.
The glum operator clang-slams the door;
ratchets the handle, engages the motor,
& with creaking jerks & jogs the counterweight,
equal to the crate-battered, work-scarred car's own,
descends.

. . . There is a motor
That is in the shaft.
There is a pulley
Hitched to the motor
That is in the shaft.
There is a rope . . .

Hum hm h*mummm*

With only the weight of their 2-man burden
for the motor to lift, *2-3*, the elevator
with creak-moaning chain, Hum hm huum*mummm*, ascends
conveys them to the uppermost floor. His gorge is
House Wrens, flurried, flushed.

Exiting is warned with a growl to watch his step.

Time now to meet the immortal magnate in his lair;
to retell his (BT's) rise from the humble; his
anecdotes & homilies, his practiced appeal.

"Any trouble getting here, Principal Washington?"
"None whatsoever, Sir, & thank you for asking,"
is how it begins.

Opens with show of his Tuskegee good works. "I
have learned," the Wizard offers the mogul, who
in his thronish high-backed leather chair rocks slightly,
like a child awaiting spooned pabulum, "that there is

a great gape between studying about things &
studying the things themselves, between book-learning
& the illumination of hands-on-work. "

His expected patron being self-made too,
understands & touts hard work's worth, nods, as
Washington, with a master-beggar's notion of
the sleight of hand that unties purse strings, confides
his hooky playing just that morning. A rare
practice he does not preach. His host, whom Colonel
Roosevelt branded a "malefactor of great wealth,"
nods, says, dry but conspiratorial, "Yes,
the occasional diversion to sharpen focus."

BT cites Griffith's 1-reelers' titles, recounts
plots' twists & turns, &, in these matters, sensitive
to mood changes as spring wind shifts to hunting hawks
on the wing, feels his host's interest rise—from detached
admiration for him (BT)—delineation
of Colored Possibility, & echoing
the capitalist's own rise from rags—to focused,
even intense connection, as BT conjures
Griffith's George like an out-of-sleeve rabbit; pulls him
forth, the prized sample from a peddler's satchel.

BT thinks of Edison: "Anything that won't sell,
I don't want to invent. Its sale is proof
of utility, and utility is success."

BT, "most useful Negro of his race in the world,"
telling how at the picture-show he had gotten
teary-eyed at the truth & moral, the moral
truth of Griffith's tales; word-fashions George till he,
like a genie from a jar, is there with them, George,
good, humble & willing, gray but not grizzled, George.
Ready at a nod to step in where needed. Good-

hearted George, who can be trusted to follow wisdom,
do best for all involved.
                    BT inferring
without saying, George is the Tuskegee student
seasoned; stout, sturdy, steady, faithful, & safe.
Never shirk or strike. The long-term investment. Top
of Tuskegee's line; . . . newer; quicker; safer; longer
lasting . . . get a good look; take your time.

Then briefly recapping his model institution's
cobbling from dirt, desire, & kindling,
& the kindness of those with foresight &
meaningful means to contribute to the uplift
of his little school, & the densely ignorant
of the race (not to mention his reputation),
BT, with a banker's demeanor & his
sorcerer's resourcefulness side-paths, to quoting
fixed & variable rates; per capita cost
per student; resources; assets & endowment
particulars.
                    Then, eyes downcast & patient,
reassured by Good George's presence (as testament,
to stir the heart, prick the conscience, & add comfort),
he waits.
                    "Everything comes to him who hustles while
he waits," BT thinks, Edison again, as a
secretary enters like a whisper, politely
reminds, the meeting has run long—only to be
brushed away by the magnate's backhand wave; before,
Thank You, Doctor Washington, a pleasure. No, sir,
thank you. & dip of pen & scrawl. & parting.
                                        Amen.

Down, sir?
Inquires the main elevator operator
in stiff livery & posture of steel. Steps in

the plush dram, cost more than a semester of
Tuskegee's teacher's salary.

Yes. Thank you.
Interior of black walnut, waxed to looking-
glass gloss, as with Mrs. Ruffner's floors, he, on hands
& knees, penitent, labored over with love, There,
in webby gray-grit skein, or, mal-focused photo-
play projection, himself, darkly—Smart, but without
show, 3-piece sack suit, band collar, crisp as snow,
bow tie, shined boots, & homburg, misshaped to hint
of humble from being hand held. Above being
taken for Zip Coon dandy, but below uppity
arrogant.
                Looks away—
                        Monopolies' name
inlaid, ivory, gold.
                        Looks back. His face,
even through polished char smudge, practiced mask of
compliance, sheathing mine-deep layers of compaction,
mirroring his viewers' desire, & what they
imagine most noble & humane in themselves.
back at them—
                        Burnished brass doors sigh shut, as the
counterweight

drops

Plip—

—There is a rope
looped over the pulley—
not
like in the Malden Mine
all those years ago,
scrunched in a scuttle

& swallowed
down
the pitch-hole
maw,
to work & wander in blind want—

—Plop—

but

drop

9 floors
like a sack of cotton
on a scale-hook.

Remembers
in his craw: a decade or so ago descent
from the 26-stories-high Chicago Worlds
Fair Ferris Wheel;
                    then,
                          in the West African hut,
housing "the racial peculiarities and
customs" of their savage kind, a tyke in ringlets
& pink; lollipop & U.S. flag on a stick,
looking from him to the Dahomeyans & back,
implored, "Will they eat us, Ma, will they?"

Booker Taliaferro Washington, safely
at the bottom of the drop,
                    plip,
                    plop, heart pounding
like waking from a dream, exits the polished box
with the polished doors, by the insistent sentry
who'd sent him to the rear. Does not gloat, goad, but nods,
& through the revolving door reels like Daniel's wheel

back into the bee-busy rush. Moves, unnoted,
just out of frame of Edison's north-looking
camera eye, preserving, for prosperity
& future study, the helter-skelter business-
district streetscape actualities.

Cowhide wallet, his embossed initials. Hand-tooled
appreciation, courtesy Class of '02,
holds, in his waistcoat's inner pocket, via
the generosity of his industrialist,
financier friend above, trust fulfilled: a cheque
with significant figures. Sum sufficient to finance
a needed laboratory. Bequeathed, with a few strokes,
to improve relations between the races, &
help his (BT's) needsome flock press forward,
through their own hard work & sacrifice.

fade out, fade in on:

Which Treats of the Stations in Life & Pursuits of the Famous Southern Gentlemen, Masters Griffith & Dixon, & of What Happens When They Sally Forth in Their Twin Tiltings against the Windmills Obstructing Their U-turn to & Recapturing of Their Imagined Age of Chivalry ("Over-Reaching Themselves" in That Regard, as Sister Ida B. Wells Will Soon Signify); & Other Events That Deserve to Be Suitably Recorded

D. W. Griffith after a few hundred
Biograph 1-reelers rife with cowering damsels,
blameless, clean & chaste, menaced by brutes with shadowed
faces tramp-tramping in places not their own, who,
in the melodramatic nick of time, in the

fancy of the day, get dished their just deserts by
moral, manly heroes. White, of course. Yes. Yes. Yes.

Exposed to the rudiments of a way of life
ravaged & left to rot, Griffith & Dixon, like
Dixie's Romulus & Remus, suckle on the
tart tits of the She Wolf of self-pity &
paranoia—If only the niggers labored
like they should—withstand & set off on their twin
but singular quests for vengeance & penance, &
like Romulus & Remus, Griffith & Dixon
home to the spot in their hearts' neglect, & find
Natalis Nation, the citadel city
on the Southern hill. A vantage point from which they
can look away, look away from the here & now
& its enshrouding cloud of drub & ruin, to look
away & turn away, & devise a way back
to Edenic Dixie-Land, the not forsaken
or forgotten land of dreams & cotton.
                                        Fired by
fear; elimination through Amalgamation;
Africanization mongrelization; race-
mixing, to put it plain: outcome of 2 evil
evils being a nation of reconstructed
blacks controlling their labor & products produced—free;

their own men, their own masters! *"Competition,"*
Dixon, stripping it to the bone, concludes.

&/so, both Griffith & Dixon, for their separate
but = reasons, know, Yes, it's the nigger's fault.
Society must be protected from *"a riot
of Africanism."*
                        &/so, on twined, twinned
dogmatic ops: Dixon: to bar, in the short term,
blacks from destroying *"the last vestiges of*

dependence on the white man for anything." &
ultimately, the out-shipping of all negroes
from A-merica. Yes.

       & Griffith: to make moving
pictures the popular art form, & the instrument
of public education. *"In one respect,"* he
says, *"nearly all pictures are good in that they show
the triumph of good over evil."* Film, says he,
functions like *"the hand of God,"* says this to sylphish
Miss Lillian Gish (1893–19-
93), nubile ingénue poster girl for
A-MERICAN Victorian sensitivity.
Gish is also in *Orphans of the Storm,*
Intolerance, & other of Griffith's epics.

Deep smitten with her; she calls him Mister Griffith.
Slapping his crop against his boot top (tap-tap) in
exact meter, while pacing, pacing, an exact
number of steps forth & back, he goes on (slap-tap)
saying, with drawled, slightly sibilate sincerity
he (tap-slap) is *"working in the universal
language that had been predicted in the Bible,"*
a language (pace-tap) *"which was to make all men brothers"*
(turn, pause) *"because they would understand each other."*
In a near whisper while leaning forward, so that
she has to incline his way, he goes on, *"This could
end wars and bring about the"* (3 beat, tap
accompanied pause) *"millennium."* She, seen by him
in close up, is flushed. Glowing. She lowers her head
a little, peruses him with dewy but deep
gaze; demurely looks away, lashes fluttering
like his heart. The crop writhes, a serpent in his
fever-dampened palm.

—By *all men,* in the above, Griffith means, as
Jefferson, Franklin, Madison, & Henry

before him meant, men of like mark, standing, =,
on elevated footing. He does not mean North
or South rabble, common crackers or yahoos, nor
jazz men, or colored men, or the like, who are,
at this serendipitous moment, taking, like
motion pictures, their first baby steps in a
flickering light of their own, toward a power
that could bring about the millennium.

In 1909 Erich von Stroheim (18-
85–1957), from Austria,
lands in New York & by1914 is crewing
on *Birth of a Nation*. Passing himself as Count
Erich Oswald Hans Carl Maria von Stroheim
und Nordenwall. Truth be told his daddy makes hats &
his ma ain't royalty. Later, when he gets his
close up, he's perfected the monocled, close-cropped
Teutonic type with sado-sinister dash, as the
"Man You Love to Hate."

Feeling his intentions mandated by the fire
of the first Revolution's founding Fathers good
& true (the cock of the roosters noted above),
Griffith, pioneering, plows on with close ups, cross-
cuts, simultaneous action, flashbacks, fade outs,
& the epic, techniques previously tools of
the page, of Prose & Rhyme. Griffith adapts Thomas
Dixon's novel *The Clansman,* makes

BIRTH OF A NATION,
(Insert advertising placard)

AN HISTORICAL ROMANCE
OF THE KU KLUX KLAN.

Premiers in Atlanta, Monday, 6 December.
At film's finale Miss Gish's character, as
with Stepin' Fetchit prior, fronts a triumphant
Rebel parade. Dramatically ratcheted here
Griffith shines light on wretched Klan. On Thanksgiving,
11 nights before, moth-bally old robes &
hooded masks creep forth from the murk of dishonor.
The South & William Joseph Simmons (1880–
1945) step out.

No, not Dr. William J. Simmons (18-
49–1890). Not the ex-slave,
& Kentucky college president before
the school is named for him. Not that one. No. Not
the educator, writer, journalist, editor
who sets up teacher training at Howard, &
becomes American National Baptist
president. No, not the one with the black skin, but
the other with the black heart, who (like Dixon, is
a former man of the cloth), stunned still, & still lost
after Divine Revolt made foul by mortal defeat,
is inspired by Dixon & Griffith's hope
of Confederate Eden's reclamation.

This Simmons, veteran of TR's Cuban dust up,
now self-dubbed Imperial Wizard, stands atop
The Peach State's Stone Mountain, ignites the signaling
blaze of a fiery cross, publicizing
the reborn Klan & the film's opening. Ads
for each appear side by side in the local press.

Saturday, 2 days before opening, the
"Organization of the Invisible Empire,
Knights of the Ku Klux Klan" is granted a state charter.
To preserve "pure Americanism" is its
motto, "Not for self but for others."

Opening day sees a robed & hooded cadre
of mounted Knights. They parade outside the Peachtree
Street theater. They fire salutes into the air.
Inside, Confederate-Gray clad ushers preside.
Griffith denies any connection between
"the organization that saved the South from the
anarchy of black rule . . . ," & his film. Yes.

*Two scenes not in the film, nor in the sweepings from
the cutting room floor: Thundering Jack is a gray ghost.
He floats like morning fog. There is no sound. Nothing moves.
There is a chill.*
　　　　*At the heart of the wooded darkness
beyond the misted meadow is darkness, restless
as sin, sullen as guilt, & black as the plague, as
fear. Yes.
Blackness.*

Birth of a Nation is ". . . arguably [?] the most
important motion picture ever made."
The critical community raves over its
portrayal of "Historic incidents," & its
"unprecedented sensitivity and beauty . . ."

Mythographic as medieval cathedral
stained-glass, the 3 hours of the Mighty Spectacle
of Birth's flickering flashes spread through darkened
venues, idealizing (Southern) American
morals, principles, aesthetics, history, &
demonizing the deviant indigenous
inferiority of coloreds.

Blacks are not, though his portrayal proves, not *just*,
as previously presented, nappy, sappy, &
slap happy. Not, he artfully authenticates,
just simple-minded, chicken-napping, crap-shooting,

whiskey-guzzling, ghost-fearing, burlesque-worthy ciphers
given to cowering postures & rolling eyes.
OH, NO. They are *not*, Griffith shouts, like *FIRE!*
in crowded theaters, just basically buffoons,
as blackened-faced minstrelsy's pre-war purveyors
had us believe!

Griffith, with his newfangled show & tell, tells—
                                                    well,
if you peep beneath the surface, see, what you see
is his blacks are not so well kept secretly soot-smudged
whites
          so, 1st of all, don't that make it just more short-
witted minstrelsy blatherskite, bosh, bull, bunkum,
gas, gup, hokum, & hooey; repackaged swag: new
patch on an old rag, moonshine as new wine,
                                                    so,
2d, don't it just muddy the message & true
meaning of his imagining, & make one wonder—
well, just what is the dark tale he's *really* telling,
trying to be selling to
                              sentimentalists,
somnambulist bleeding-heart Democrats; that
these neo-post-bellum blacks aren't *only* buffoons.

See them he says, pointing with his riding crop while
trying to keep his mask of outraged manhood from
slipping with his other (his under?) hand, see them,
as the degenerate, brutish, lascivious,
low-down, coonish goonish goon coons of many loath-
some & lovable parts; the Cain's black seed they
really are. & uncontrolled, Griffith artfully
illustrates, with righteous bombast, they *will* revert,
become a beastly band of unruly Dark
Savages, with black designs on Civilization,

Teutonic Ideals, partisan Anglo-Saxon
privilege, & White womanhood.

(But, oh, do you David Llewelyn Wark, knoweth
the true nature of the 2-faced beast ye harbor
on thy ark?)

(cross-cut
to a " Historic incident" from the film:)
a visualization of Emancipation's consequence:
the floor of a "Reconstruction" era
Southern State House:
Congress in session:
aswarm with shiftless,
pork chop-gnawing, goober-
eating, packaged whiskey-sipping, toe-picking
carpetbagger-controlled coon legislators
lording it over

(Insert Title Card)

> **"THE HELPLESS WHITE MAJORITY"**

while in the gallery popinjay darkies, like
apes at supper, guffaw & knee-slap in primal
jubilation. Apery at their japery.
Evidence in black & white (or is it white in
black): power in the hands of any but "free white
persons" is a shortcut to political,
sexual, moral corruption & chaos:

Long shot: moonlit night:
Anglo-Saxon knights-errant, hooded & robed, charge
to the rescue on spurred steeds, their ghostly flowing

vestures cloaking, beneath the symbol of purity,
the temper of their hard-riding, wrong-righting mission
to save the present nostalgia, or some distressed
damsel.

"Instead of saving one poor little Nell," Griffith
says, "this [3 hour 15 reeler: 68
thousand People, 3thousand horses, 8 months
in the making" work] will be a ride "to save a
nation."

Would asking from "what, or for whom" be rhetorical?

18 February: close up:
Woodrow Thomas Wilson in the White House:
history scholar, political scientist,
high-minded son of a Presbyterian
minister, adulterer, President of the
United States of A-merica.

Like flames, the lights & shadows dance in the darkened
room as Griffith's film is screened for the especial
amusement of the President, cabinet members,
& friends . . .

Wilson, 1902–10 Princeton U. President;
1911–'13 Garden State Governor; '13–
'21 U.S. President, self-proclaimed
"instrument of God" (& former classmate
of Thomas Dixon, Jr., "red-blooded" populist
author of *The Clansman,* the work on which the film
is based). Wilson, who, in 1865,
8 years old (a late to learn reader—not till 10),
at the side of his bereft, clinch-jawed, pro-South
Presbyterian preacher daddy, sees Union
Johnnies parade chained Jefferson Davis, deposed
head of the Lost Cause, flip-flopped, slumped-down, spun-around

Confederacy, in a creaking wagon like
a common criminal, or—slave, through Augusta's
streets, en route to the pokey. Wilson praises
Birth of a Nation as ". . . history written in
Lightning . . . it is all so terribly true,"
he declares.

           "Rule of reason" Chief Justice Edward
Douglass White (1845–1921),
son of the sugar plantation Thibodaux
Louisianans, sees it, his 1st, the next night
with some of the other boys from the court. White had
been a member of the Klan.

              & still later
Wilson asserts in his *History of the A-*
merican People, that the Klan stemmed the overthrow
of Civilization & the attempt "to put
the white South under the heel of the black South."
The next stop, it goes unnecessarily said,
Miscegenation.

They (Wilson, Dixon, Griffith, & their ilk) believe
the film, its way lighted by "The Fiery Cross
of the Ku Klux Klan," is a "diversion
to the masses," & a recruitment tool for the
Democratic Party. Public school children,
Griffith predicts, "will never be obliged to read
history again." With the birth of these notions
Birth of a Nation opens. & in a brilliant
lightning stroke Griffith (once again via the
"entertainment" Industry) brings forth on this new
nation, a Pop Theology (the re-cast A-
merican consumer Myth of Noble
Vigilantism), conceived in fear,
& dedicated to the proposition
that all good A-merican FREE WHITE PERSONS
defend the rocky ramparts of Anglo-

Saxonism against all hints of the huddled
darkness, largely noted & long remembered,
at the hallowed heart of their conscience's night;
the possibility of negro's humanity
& worthfulness.

They sit in the dark illuminated by Mr.
Griffith's reassuring anthem:

"Coons
IS
goons, &
we ain't."

Best to fear them, our Superiority affirms,
& goes forward, spirits restored, they reason, than
face the firing squad of the possibility
of their similarity! Lawd a' mussy &
thank you Mr. Griffith!, for your silent but vital
& oh so compellingly eloquent epic.

IT IS A HIT. It is a runaway hit. It is a
box office bonanza. Celluloid gold.

Due to Griffith's handiwork it dawns on others
that flickers are more than mere eye-popping Pabulum.
Pap for populi. It has prospects. Promise far
beyond box office receipts. Handled with care it
is an inclusive venue for the party's-lines
reaching the vulgar, the vile, the low lowest's
common ear, heart, mind, & purse; those far removed
from the refined & finite possibilities
of the exclusive Finer Arts: theater,
symphonies, & ballet, reserved for the select,
the singular.
            Following showings:

RIOTS COUNTRY WIDE
MANY COLORED INJURED

& in the economic & aesthetic
excitement cinema's Color Line is drawn.
Hollywood has its artistic & racial template
for the coming century, & beyond.

& the up beat down beat strikes up the band,
the rich get richer, the poor need more,
2, THREE, 4 & Time & the Press & Church
& State & the A-merican populace
consumer, the A-mericanists
Forward March, as the band plays on.

"La Seranata," or "Angel's Serenade," by
Gaetano Braga, 1829–
1907, is sampled by Joseph
Carl Breil, 1870–1926,
Griffith's music man, as *Birth of a Nation*'s main
theme. It later, in another revolting
development, becomes the basis for the
Amos & Andy theme. & the band plays on.

In the meantime, across the Color Line, negroes:
Blue-Veins, blue-blacks, & of every trade, shade &
stripe, unite against *Birth of a Nation*. Kidnapping,
slavery, Jim Crow, & lynching, now this.
They protest, picket, & parade.

Of What Happens When
Birth of a Nation Comes to Tuskegee

Tuskegee, Alabama, Assembly Hall.

Unease rises like methane gas in marsh or mine.

The Birth of a Nation:
Or The Clansman.

Griffith Feature Films
produced exclusively
by D. W. Griffith

The theater's dark dredges up BT's time down
Malden Mine. At work-day's end pulleyed from pit's
soot-black dank rankness, toward shaft's mouth; like whimed up
from a dream; blinking through his slated fingers
against day's fulgent light—

　　　　　　　　　　　　or, in another dream,
his glare up through a deck-grate from a slave ship's hold.

> "If in this work we have conveyed to the mind
> the ravages of war to the end that war
> May be held in abhorrence,
> this effort will not have been in vain."

In his opening plea for Motion Picture art
Griffith demands as his right "to show the dark side
of wrong"; "illuminate the bright side of virtue . . ."

Around BT, Tuskegee's teachers, students, &
staff know this is something new, not (this time) only
to them, but the wide world way beyond Tuskegee,
Alabama. They don't know to trust this picture play,
but not wanting to be seen country by those
among them might be savvied to this spectacle,
are uncertain as to the correctness of, or
expectations as to their conduct or response.

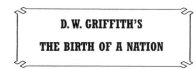

> **D. W. GRIFFITH'S**
> **THE BIRTH OF A NATION**

BT clears his throat for silence from the student
section's ironic snickers & muffled hisses.
He is not heard by all above the piano
playing of Mathematics Instructor, Professor
Lyons, pressed into service to provide music
as the film unfolds. The unruly too are hushed
or nudged to attention.

"The bringing of the African to America,"
the placard reads, "planted the first seed of disunion."

Lindsey whispers, "Now our fault they brought us here!"
Smothered laughs. Hissed *Shhsss!*

Principal Washington slowly rises from his
front row center seat. Faces them. Light & shadows
jig like marionettes across the proscenium
of his body & face; eyes, red-rimmed, wet with fatigue,
burn in the darkness like a miner's carbide lamp.

Mute they watch Africans bondaged; Negro & Northern
abolitionists; white Southern family life play
across & behind him. Stifled laughter answers
a muffled retort. "If you cannot conduct
yourselves like Tuskegee students," he begins,
as the film father, "the kindly master" casually
drops a cat on a lazing pup. Grumbles among
the pupils. "Low down old white man," someone says.
The Sage turns, looks, then looks back, an angry tremor
in his voice twinning the one in his right hand &
the more rapid, tired eye blink, blink, warns, "one more
& I will have this contraption turned off, & send
you all to quarters."

Their silence as pre-war South plays on. He sighs, turns,
his hand fumbles for the chair arm. Sits, his breathing
shallow. Margaret, Lady Principal, lays her hand
on his, leans her comforting shoulder against him.

Reels spin:
                        & they find themselves patting or nodding
at smatterings & catches of Professor Lyons's
rhythms & melodies tickling the mechanics
of their ears & feet, as Stoneman & Cameron
interfamily romances bud or wilt, or
slaves fresh from cotton picking jig & frisk—& they,
in spite of warnings & themselves gasp or cringe,
laugh in embarrassment or wily wisdom, cry out,
talk one to another or at Griffith's flickering
frieze of paranoia & vigilante revenge.

Lyons weaves strains, variations, & inversions
of quadrilles, waltzes, spirituals, rags, marches,
classical airs & arias — seria & buffa —
reels, cantatas, recitatives, each in its own
tempo beneath this new-century wonder they're
witnessing. Few question if he's paying any
mind to Griffith's story or its point.

For long stretches he doesn't play. Sits. Half turned
from the screen, or leaning forward. Concentrating
on the sheet music before him they assume
is the proper score.
                    With up-flick of tongue tip &
middle finger down flip wetting the tip to flip
the page, as if scanning a newspaper, then,
without obvious prompting from page or screen,
again begins.

War is in the air. Lincoln signs proclamations.
Men join departing regiments.

Gray & Blue clash. Rebellion battle scenes:
silent booms, billowing smoke, blood-hot dumb shrieks,
& fires of war, as their fate (long decided)
once again titters in the balance.
                              Private
tragedies. & the South falls.
                         Honest Abe, the Great
Rail Splitting, Emancipating, Mister President
Abraham Lincoln falls.

Their silence is not hushed — but abated; the breaths
of children crouched in a candlelit stormcellar
as wind, in its full bombasity, screaks jape-mouthed,
horrisonous, hurling unsecured limbs laundry
pails chickens shingles — like toys in a 3-year-olds'

tantrum; its detritus rolling rattling banging
about the loosely latched over-head doors.

                               Lyons,

parental, reassures, playing a familiar
scrap of a bluesy but upbeat motif,
worrying it like a puppy with a rag,
shaking, tossing. Composing, recomposing
subtracting adding multiplying signaling
whispering reminding with its hint of the
forbidden devilish low-down likely putting them
in mind of evening drag-marches of home-coming cows
or old mule in a half lope toward its supper oats;
or rambling out Saturday noon then
wobbling & weaving back just before day, lap-legged
—till satisfied or in pursuit moves on.

Man! Lindsey thinks, Professor Lyons (who'd confided
in private *we* invented math while they daubed in mud
& slit goats' throats so oats would grow) is playing
outright & pure denunciation against Griffith's
every notion. His music is jooking, jiving,
jabbing, counterpunching like Jack Johnson!
It's the Manly Art of Self-Defense; geometry
of lengths, areas, & volumes of manhood right
on his piano. Keeping the taint of this cracker's
pictures off us. Just like Champion Jack wards off
White Hope yahoos! A punching combination
of their own highfaluting stuff & our Sunday
spirituals—the likes of "Don't Be Weary Traveler,"
&, "My Lord, My Lord." Even I know them.

Telling us don't get so rapt up in Griffith's new-
notioned trickery till we forget mother wit.
Telling us for all its wow & hurrah, the more
it unreels the more it's just more the same old
pitiless, unreal Jim Crow wrassles & hassles

keeping up with the times. A new-day way to get
their blood up. A spur for whites' hunting party fun
filmed; night-fire boogieman tales for whites' frightful
delight. It bears out the (true) brand of their Valor,
as they call it, the undercover cunning
in overcoming their failed Rebellion, as they call it,
to overcome Reconstruction's set-backs, & the (stained)
Purity, as they call it, of their (debased) Honor,
as they call it, & Purpose. But it's no purer,
or more honorable, Lyons playing declares,
than pigs scuffling, snuffling, snorting after scraps & slops.

& would only the most learn'ed ear—were there white
musicologists here—hear, in the time allowed,
& with the attention needed, decipher the
multi-meanings & connections in Lyons's &
Champion Jack's separated but synchronized,
syncopated sounds & poundings, saying, if some-
thing's wrong it's them, or us, not Time. There is no wrong
time. We just got to see & hear it, for what it is.

On screen, blacks, to whites' distress, rise, & worse, to whites
distress; rule, as depicted, like dastardly,
legislating interlocutors, like
revengeful minstrels.

Louisa posture perfect, handkerchief crumpled
in her palm, hands lightly in her lap. Between Charles
Lee & Lindsey, rivals, in their minds, to court her,
whisper dreams, affections, plans.

If I'm Lindsey's mate he'll guard me from life's tests &
toil. I'll do no madam's laundry or lay tables,
will strive in tandem with him.
                              & Charles Lee with his
Du Bois airs is light-skinned, will secede, succeed.

Lindsey's future will be honed on a different
grindstone. Will wrestle all comers, give good as he gets.

Just like men, Louisa thinks, as bad as the Wizard,
who sells me (women) short to raise our worth, &
in the bargain denies us Cicero, Shakespeare,
wants us auxiliaries: in service trades, or
classroom bound. Acts as if the Problem is theirs alone
to solve. Ida B. Wells-Barnett (Iola)
worries overmuch about men. But what respect
is she garnering for herself & us, stay-back,
double disenfranchised witnesses to their run
at manhood, bloody manhood. Why are theirs the only
heads fit to fill with fight or fancy? Why can't I,
as easily & justly as whites be Hermes
or Artemis, or, even, a female Ares
like my "Iola," "Valued by the Lord," Ida B.?

Like a prey-eyeing, tree top circling hawk, Charles Lee
gawks over classmates' barbered & combed naps
at the stretched-sheet screen. Peers, not for the unreeling
kinetic novels' amusements, but for tip-offs
to the ways of the people portrayed.   Another
step in his plot, he thinks—not so much to desert
the racial fields of infertile soil, whose sole yield
has been cankered crops, but to take advantage
of his gift from the gods—brown-blue eyes, buttermilk
complexion, corn-silk locks—& meld into the world
whose hubris, & policy of take & remake,
without apology or qualm, has hatched high
civilization from wilderness & muck. &
whose doers of those deeds, unjust in the doing,
cruel in the outcome, are not stoned at the gate, but
are anointed kings, & repay the weak & meek's
suspirations & lamentations with rebukes;

argumentum ad hominem, attacking
the cast-downs' meager circumstance as evidence
& justification for their woebegone ways.

Who, if they could, would not pass as one among them,
demi-demons though they are.

Louisa muses, Whites think themselves, & want us
to think them, gods. Higher Heroes. Zeus. Apollo.
Ares. & think their women Aphrodites,
Demeters, Hestias. Idle rulers of love
& punishment in a Confederate pantheon
above the world & mortal doings.

They watch Flora, sprightly young thing, with rebel flag
for sash, & innocent as a fawn, go against
her brother's warning, to fetch a pail of water.
Finds herself hotly pursued through trees & thicket
by an awful brute-black negro (a square-jawed white
in black face) newly manumitted & turned
renegade. Convinced he has dastardly designs
on her dainty virtue fair Flora scrambles up
a rocky precipice & arms spread tumbles off.

Fool, thinks Louisa. Fling your silly self away
at hint of trouble's bud. No better for you, you
& the myth-mad scalawag clot-plotted frightened
fantasies bloomed into the pampered pet you were.

My Ida B., when told to cede her train seat
she'd paid 1st class for, refused. & the moment
the mean ol' conductor put his hand on her
she fastened her teeth in it, & feet braced clung
to the seat with all her might. It took a force of 3
to eject her. She like Sojourner sued & won.

When I spread my arms, she tells them, will be to fly
not t'ward some massa's *heab'n,* but to Olympus.
& if my wing wax thaws to water, & flailing
I fall, oh well, at least I flew. Beware below!

BT
Headache. Again. Temples pounding. Strike-Ring. Pounding.
The heaving, arrhythmic locomotive
respiration of wheels clack-click-clacking 'cross
Mason's & Dixon's Line, boundary, North to South,
slave state from free, since the Missouri Compromise;
Pennsylvania to Maryland, heading home. Plip.
Clack-click-clacking & opened-throttled squeal of wheels'
dry friction, grinding on rails & fluttering in
BT's belly cavern like the whistle-screeching
House Wren.
            The feeling, a sudden start in his heart,
& headache triggered, like the lock on a strong box
snapping shut, Plop, with razor clarity (this time)
by Professor Lyons's musical figure:
syncopated trills & prattles rising then dropping,
                    drip,
                    drop,
                    plop,
                    plip—
above a clack-clicking tempo, to a fast ending
flurry beneath the Little Colonel returning
to his ruined home.

Henry B. Walthall, the Little Colonel, here
will play former Reb & town preacher in the
Rogers/Fetchit Post-Bellum *Judge Priest.*

BT, to ease the feeling, breathes deep, slow sighs.
                                            Note
to Lyons: next time tame the raw & brash. Tune it

down to the calm of choir songs in chapel, or
old Negro melodies concertized in recitals
provided during his travels by thoughtful hosts,
who in their kindness seek to free him of the stress
of travel & pecuniary cares with
soothing spiritual renditions from local
Coloreds with old-time talent—music restful &
reassuring; a joy of order & connection
for all concerned.

& as for Griffith—has betrayed himself &
us. *This,* he, weary, thinks, outmodes minstrelsy, &
naysays Kindness or Hope, is, plain as leopard spots,
the Progressive Age's new assault; the modern mock.
My "patient, faithful, law-abiding, unresentful"
way—& the steadfast course of my life's work—are this
photo-play's twin trophies, hung—

> drip,
> drop,
> plop,
> plip—

to drain. My donors will not endorse us
rewritten as blood-threats, or more than 3/5ths men.

Charles Lee, on Louisa's right, watches Reconstruction
re-created:

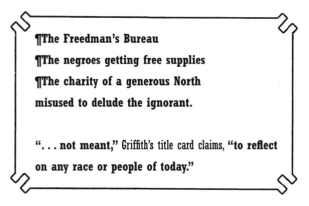

¶The Freedman's Bureau
¶The negroes getting free supplies
¶The charity of a generous North
misused to delude the ignorant.

". . . not meant," Griffith's title card claims, "to reflect
on any race or people of today."

Well it does, Charles Lee thinks, it reflects on the most
backward & hindered of the race. Susceptible
to the schemes of Northern scallywags & carpet-
baggers who strive, as President Wilson writes,
"to cozen, beguile, and use the negroes . . ." into
going on the dole, be banjo-picking, juba-
dancing rascals & scamps raising dust, but cropless,
as a way to spank the South & keep it prostrate;
gobbling up free goodies like hogs in a river
of acorn slops. Oh, my people, my backward people.

Professor Carver, needles clicking, knits & purls.
Thinks:

FALLOW:
To plow, harrow, and break up, as land, without seeding,
for the purpose of destroying weeds and insects,
and rendering it mellow. [1913 Webster]

WEED:
Any plant growing in cultivated ground
to the injury of the crop or desired
vegetation, or to the disfigurement
of the place; an unsightly, useless, or
injurious plant. [1913 Webster]

> ¶The Ku Klux Klan, the organiza-
> tion that saved the South from the
> anarchy of black rule, but not without
> the shedding of . . . blood . . .

Mary, Mary quite contrary . . .

On screen there is peril. A puerile way of life
is under siege. Washed in red, venomous buds rise

out of night's undergrowth.

How does your garden grow?

Sits sad eyed at the regermination, rooting,
& growth to blossoming of the evil rebirth
of unholy Knights of the night. Renewed with fresh
purpose, they quietly group, a squirm of maggots
suckling on sweet defeat.

With Silver Bells, And Cockle Shells,
Sing cuckolds all in a row.

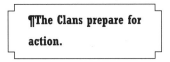
¶The Clans prepare for action.

Their need for a one-crop system of hatred,
Carver thinks, yields stunted roots & cankered fruit
from fields of exhausted, infertile, pest-ridden,
erosion-prone soil, & frustration at each
passing season's diminishing returns from their
want to trample, gain, & dictate.

The meek, as his bible tells him, shall inherit
the earth, & gather the lilies of the field.

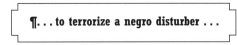
¶. . . to terrorize a negro disturber . . .

Their horses prancing at the thought of getting to
gallop, the Invisible Empire of sham
Aryans, in a mad dash, are off.

Had it really happened; this how it really was?
Carver wonders. A Klan kidnapping begins his
biography & he believes it—but had been

but a babe, & at best his recall is a blur,
dimmed, crude confusion, half-lit shadows & wooly
sounds—& perhaps a scream.

Pictures himself swaddled, 2 years old (him older
now by twice than mother would then have been). Thinks
at times it is hooves, & at others his ear
against the drumming of her breast, but when he tries
to call it clearer it irises down, until,
like the end of a film episode, it is but
a pinprick of light, then even that is gone.

If he did not know better, had not, as he &
his mother had, been up-wretched, kucluckled, swept off
in a stampede of ghost-white on steamy stallions;
if they had not been converts into the barnyard manure
of the Klan's cultus of fear, or if he did not
know the bullying that is their intent, &
butchery of its outcome, he might be thrilled by
their on-screen, heart-thundering charge, shrouded in
billowing robes & dunce-cone headwear, crosses, torches,
& guns aloft, on their self-appointed mission
to preserve all they hold American, holy,
& white.

Later he will quiz them. Who knows the parable
of the weeds in the field? Will explain, as Jesus
had to his disciples. The field is the world.
The sower of the good seed is the Son of Man.
The good seeds are the purest sons of The Kingdom.
The sower of weeds is the devil, & those weeds
his sons. At the end of the age, the Son of Man's
disciples will weed out His Kingdom & cast them
into the fiery furnace. ". . . where there will be
weeping and gnashing of teeth. Then the righteous will
shine like the sun in the kingdom of their Father.

He who has ears, let him hear" (Matthew 13:
24–30, 36–43).
"God took man and put him in the Garden to work it
and take care of it. And God commanded man,
'You are free to eat from any garden tree; but
do not eat from the knowledge tree of good and evil,
for when you eat of it you will surely die.'"

& ruled in the garden, naming & tending-to
in that time before the confusions of
companionship & temptation & the damning
knowledge of self & of the sin that sowed.

Remembering:
                    a darting from under-leaf.
Skink eating Scarlet King snake. Banded red & yellow,
". . . red on yellow, kill a fellow." & before God's
6th Commandment takes hold the hoeblade strikes & His
slinky creature is in His kingdom.

LINDSEY
Knows nothing of music past Sunday spirituals
shouted to the sky, field hollers flung like chaff
against the wind, & nighttime's moans.
                                 Too voice-awkward
to try to sing—but sits wet-eyed, open-hearted
when Louisa lifts her head, & her voice wells up
in amidst the swelling choirs, yes he does.

LOUISA
When she, strolling, her parasol atwirl along
the Continent's *strassen* & *rues,* boulevards
& promenades, humming tunes from a rainbow of—
European white men's volumes of musics
she doesn't know the names or forms of (but will) &
that will wash over her evenings in the concert halls;

evenings she isn't doing her true woman's work,
calling out, in public forums, against the horrors
of Negro women's defamation; her presence, words,
& knowledge of the world & its ways
refutation of any notion of colored
women's inferiority.

Yes. It is her expectation she will hear full
& fully orchestrated renditions of all
of these hints Professor Lyons, in his haste, only
samples, like bonbons from a red velvet box.

MISS WATERS
Admiration & jealousy at his worldly thoughts,
& being able—as man, mathematician
& musician—to speculate & question,
& without a woman's restraint, give vent to feelings,
maudlin or merry, gay or grieving. Just the thought
of that degree of freedom is enough to make
her cry.
          In self-whispers she aches to wipe his sweat
with her lace-edged hankie, then fan it out, gentle
as moonlight, warm & damp upon her breast.

G.W.C.
Young Lyons—as if after collecting samples,
one each, on campus & off, he returns & places
his floral jamboree in a single vase bouquet,
as if division, class, family, or genus
makes no never mind.

MISS WATERS
All the while Professor Lyons (Jefferson) has been
doing as we (wish to) do when no one (our esteemed
Founder, say, or whitefolks) is around: course &
meander along beneath, with, behind, ahead,

like water seeking its own level. Not having
to curtsey to master's pomp or prepotency.
He—Jefferson, like a mannish boy, shoulders privies
till they tilt & topple, chunks dirt clumps against barn sides
for the glee of earth bombs burst.

Lift Every Voice and Sing,
                              "Stony the road we trod,
Bitter the chastening rod . . ."
                              Jefferson plays as we,
the lights on,   *"Thou who has brought us thus far*
on the way"
                    collect ourselves, stand & stretch & in
orderly, Tuskegee fashion, clear the hall,
                                        "Thou
who has by Thy might Led us into the light,"
quietly singing or humming along,
                              "Keep us
forever in the path, we pray . . ."

Cunning as a vixen, I, in distant *pas de deux,*
time my steps with his.

& if I (still) am not calculating enough
to (accidently) walk out with him I'll quicken
my step, & nervous as an aspen, stop him,
my hand, lightly (politely) on his arm, catch &
hold his eye, refract rebuffs he's used to ward
the others off, & say, to him, The snap of your
syncopations is salve, if not shield, against
hateful blaze of *Birth of a Nation*'s inventive,
insulting assault with bullwhip intent to trigger
our wonder; shock & humiliation in its
footage's every inch. Thank him, hiding my
trembling hand by twisting, not overmuch I hope,
my hankie. Say how much his music (he,

I'll mean) is inspiration to our students (me,
I'll mean). Say it tells them they are still the hope
of all who (helped) send them here: mamas & daddies
& big mamas & granddaddies, & them, &
neighborhoods & communities & towns. Say, not too
in a rush I hope, It is the sass, & bad
nigger-ness when he plays that quickens our pulse &
steels our spines. See what he says—with his gruff &
grumbly self—to that.

Acknowledging passing greetings with nods &
half smiles Principal & Lady Principal
Washington make their deliberate cross-campus
walk home to the Oaks, a bath, his bed—where sleep is
a blueblack nightmare; boxed in the casket of his
compromise, unable to raise voice or hand
in protest, twists & twists.

"You know," he says "I will permit no man
to narrow and degrade my soul by making me
hate him." "As you have said, dear."

In a confiding tone he says, "Dixon or Griffith,
one or the other, it matters not which, says, 'one
purpose of that photo-play was to create
a feeling of abhorrence, especially among
white women, against colored men.'" "Hummm," is her reply.

"& Dixon, I'm certain it is he, says he hopes
to have Negroes removed from America, &
hopes the show we just saw helps to accomplish that."

"Thomas Dixon. He thinks coloreds ever lowly,
me included." Margaret clucks. "Denies us any
contribution to human progress." He pauses
like Adam on the 6th evening, to survey their

surroundings. She understands with a nod. "The South,"
he continues, "for all its advantages has
produced—who, what of lasting achievement, to hold up
& declare magnificent?"
                          She, worried nearly
to distraction at his weight loss, headaches, slowed stride,
squeezes his arm; her answer.

In sight of the amber-saffron glow of the Oaks'
windows in the Alabama night.

"Yet they fear, in their loudest tones, I'll no longer
train types who'll continue taking their 'rightful lowly
place,' but school eventual equals who will, with
thoughts of lust & loins & mongrel offspring converse
with white wives & women clerks."

They begin again, almost up the path to their porch.
"The white South beats its breast like an ape king, yet is
backward as Africa's baboons. 'To hold a man
down, you have to stay down with him.'" "So you've said, dear."
"Repeating myself aren't I?" "You're tired," she consoles.
"Not too tired to remember a few months after
word of my sitting down with Colonel Roosevelt,
a manuscript arrived by post." He pauses.
They are at the foot of the 6-step rise. She waits,
deciding against calling for the boys to come aid
their father. *The Leopard's Spots, A Romance of the
White Man's Burden—1865 to 1900*,
by *Mister* Dixon," he says. Irony in her
sharp exhale. "With a note. I paraphrase, 'I hope
you will enjoy it, and if you can find time
to say a word in review I will very much
appreciate it.'" Lets him catch his breath before
she says, "The vilifying rascal." Then asks, "Was
there a cheque enclosed?" They laugh. He shakes his head.

"Dixon did, later offer, for Tuskegee's coffers,
10thousand if I'd disavow all aspirations
toward social equality." "The nerve," she says.
They laugh. Pause. With a catch in her voice she calls out
for Booker T. Jr., and Ernest, the boys.

Hope, he thinks.
Hope.
Hope.
Hope is all I had.

Hope:

All I had.

A sweet given in kindness for a chore well done
to dissolve lingering coaldust caking the tongue
after descending each day & rising out of
impossible darkness is all I had. All there
is.

All left.

1915
Dat Famous Chicken Debate, a play of the blackface
variety poking pointed fun at Du Bois
(University of Africa) v.
Washington (Bookertea College) by centering
on the questionable criminality
of niggers stealing chickens, thus proving their dust up
isn't just an in the family ruckus.
Its point, after all the dimwitted, thick-tongued
hilarity, is lynching is (still) the penalty
for black lawbreaking. Its author, Walter Long, is
Birth of a Nation's blackened face, damsel-threatening-

gets-his-just-deserts-at-the-end-of-a-Klan-rope-
brute, Gus. Long, in life praised from every quarter as a
gentleman of the first water, he goes on to
costar as a comic bad guy foil for Misters
Laurel & Hardy.

24

Wherein Is Related the Rush of Defenders to Griffith's Defense . . . Along with Other Events to Do with Mr. Mayer

Griffith says & shows, "There is nothing, absolutely
nothing, calculated to raise the goose-flesh
on the back of an audience more than that
of a white girl in relation to Negroes."

But, Griffith's Legions, his generation's best minds:
journalists, logicians, clerics, savant pedagogues,
promoters, financiers, & theorists, squat like
Phoenicians, or fallen angels, on Hell's precipice,
& deaf to the cries of the sacrificed,
dispassionately toss reason & judgment
on the ever-burning flames of the furnace
of craving that is his audience's need for
the nourishment of the affirmation of their
Supremacy before it.

They declare *Birth* an Aesthetic Triumph!
an Instant Classic! Masterpiece! Mr. Griffith,

they argue, is "the Shakespeare of the screen," & surely
if there are "inflammatory excesses" or
"racial overtones," he is simply a victim
of his isolation, being far removed from
urbane enlightenment as he is in this
Gehennaian Hollywood. It's his innocence,
his naïveté, his genius, they justify, fuels
his inflamed images. It's his God-given right,
they exhort, to give the audience "what they want"
& how they want it as the old minstrel song says,
&, to show "the dark side of wrong," "illuminate
the bright side of virtue . . ."

'Tis Shakespeare, first put an English-speaking black
on the British boards: Aaron, a Moor & villain,
figure of vice, & the beloved of Tamora,
Goth Queen in *Titus A.*

The unleashed sack of stormwind endorsements, & waves
& wake of their verbiage inundates, sweeps away
before it, without abatement, all vessels
of objection; not like loner Elijah to the
heaven of equality, but like Ulysses
into a seemingly boundless, boiling sea
of segregation & exclusion.
       Yea, see
the tossed-about "sea washed" hands, including Du Bois,
at the tiller of the good ship N DOUBLE A
C P. *Birth of a Nation* is "the meanest
vilification of the Negro race," they say,
riding out the wrath in their storm-pelted rafts
of righteousness.

Birth of a Nation indeed signals the blazing
rebirth of the reconstructed Ku Klux Klan.

To restore "100% American-
ism" the Klan's Lost Cause culturist agenda
is swathed in Ol' Glory, & the mantle of
Christianity. Is sold as American born
Protestantism. Is a recruitment tool for
frustrated whites (South & North). No others need apply.
Blacks, back-sliding whites, Jews, Roman Catholics,
foreigners, anti-traditionalists, &
immoralists, continue as baby seals
to the bludgeons of Klan "family values" invective.
Its appeal appeals. Its fear fits fearsome whites
to a T; parties & socials spread like wildfire.
Flocks flock. Klan rolls soar: 100thousand recruits
in a year.

A congressional investigation uproots
nothing. Sheets are unruffled. No one is unmasked.

The K.K.K. song is triumphantly sung to
the tune of "A Hot Time in the Old Town To-night."

Iris out.
Fade in.

1915 still:
long shot: a Boston motion picture theater.
close up: Louis Burt Mayer, a.k.a. Eliezer,
or Lazar (Louis B.) Mayer, its owner, b.,
according to his official bio, 4 July,
1885.
T'aint that just Yankee Doodle Dandy, but a lie
by about a year & some . . . & by a Lazar,
or Eliezer Meir, or some such, out of
Minsk, Belarus—Russia, escaping his Cossack-
ridden home in the late '80s
through England & Canada to Massachusetts.
At 19 Louis B., or L.B., recently

a junk man's son, begins, in hustler minstrelsy
tradition, to re-form himself, & there being
no business like show business he boards the
entertainment ethnic-immigrant express
to cross that divide to Full White Personhood.
Diversifies. Buys theaters, until he owns
the largest chain in New England. Exhibits
only "high quality films." Distributes
Birth of a Nation in his chain. Under-reports
the box office take. Makes a huge profit. Makes this
his move-to-Hollywood-&-make-movies money.
Becomes Hollywood's most powerful magnate.
His company houses "more stars than there are
in the heavens."
                    "Isn't God good to me?" he says,
reshuffling the deck; making the game his own.
Gives the public what it wants by picturing
the American Dream as wholesome escapism
wrapped in the Stars & Stripes.

Louis B.'s last words before his credits roll
are reportedly, "Nothing matters."

Fade out.

Cross-cut to flashback:

1915.
Havana. Jack Johnson who's had an answer
for all they've called forth — out thinking, out fighting, out
hustling & out muscling, is too fast, too brash, too
much man for their every plan, till (after
exhaustive negotiations with U.S. agents —
it's a long, slinking, stinking, weaselly, serpentine
story totally without honor, of quisling
pols, colluder clergymen, bully of judges,
bureaucrats, the public, their blue-nosed wives &

mistresses in a buzzing, nipping, nibbling, picking,
pecking conspiratorial swarm, thick as flies
on the moldering remains of their reprisal)
Jack vs. the 105-degree heat &
245-pound, 6foot6 & ½
inch, Pottawatomie Giant, Jess Willard—"If
they make white hopes any bigger," Jack cracked,
"I'll have to get stilts." In round 26, the fix in, his back
on the canvas, shading his eyes from the event's
overwhelming whiteness, is brought to heel.
         If
wearing down is the same as beating. Willard,
in denial, quips, "If Johnson throwed it, I wish
he'd throwed it sooner."
      Once counted out Jack's let back
in the good ol' US of A to serve his time
as a white slaver.
     James Weldon Johnson declares
"it was the fight of one lone black man against the world."
Calls Jack, "the perfect athlete," whose "bad personal breaks
deprived him of the sympathy and approval
of most of his own race," yet, "his record as a
pugilist has been something of a racial asset."
Sticking & jabbing, Johnson continues, "The white
race, in spite of its vaunted civilization,
pays more respect to the argument of force
than any other race in the world. . . . [Jack] not only
looked the white man in the eye, but hit him in the eye."

31 years early, it was the perfect
obituary for the Champ, who in
'46, speeding, dies.
      Thomas Dixon, same year,
a court clerk, an invalid, dies too.

Fade out.
Iris in.

Is Devoted to a Description of BT's Final Sally; His Homecoming, His Last Encounter with His Arch Nemesis, & His Last Considerations & Reconsiderations

"Success is to be measured not so much by the position that one has reached in life, as by the obstacles which he has overcome while trying to succeed."—Booker T. Washington

Going
down.

BT, bone-weary, departs New York with Margaret
& doctor, heading home. "I was born in the South
have lived all my life in the South . . ."

       Rock-sway.

South.

Home.

Plip.

"The Gos-pel train is a'comin' I hear it just at
hand,"

Health failing.

"I hear the car wheel rumblin'
And rollin' through the land.

Jim Crow car. The doctor. Margaret. Hold his hand. Stroke
his brow. Hot.
                Going down. Slow. Pass shacks. Weary. Slack.
"Get on board
little chil-dren, Get on
board, children, .
Get on board little children,
For there's room for ma-ny a ma-ny a more."

Muybridge-like flickering-frieze: setting sun's flames flash
in syncopated snatches through trees trees trees trees,
like shutters tripped by the locomotives passing.

Along the tracks, wraithish blacks, silent as smoke, hear
wheels & steel's rail music, see framed lantern-light reel
& rock through the night.
                Hum hm h*mummm*
                      2-3-hummm

Blanket's edges tucked tight. The night threatens rain
that does not fall. Sleep too threatens, does not come.

Jim Crow, Jim Crow . . .

Going down
slow. Morning. Noon. Night. "Next stop . . ."

"I hear the bell and whis-tle, The com-ing round the
curve";

Rushing countryside. Hovels. Depots. Livestock. Crossroads.

"She's playing all her steam and pow'r   And strainin' ev'ry nerve."

Trees. Trees. Trees.
                    "Get on board, chil-dren,"

Plop.

"Get on board, chil-dren,"

Thinks:
"From the time that I can remember anything,
almost every day of my life has been
occupied in some kind of labor."

"Get on
board, children," 8million trying to say something.
To him. Rushing by. Something he cannot hear.

Life of punching a hole through a rock, rock 'size of
a mountain, mountain black as coal, coal old as life.

"For there's room for ma-ny a more."

Builder; fund raiser; broker. From (almost) nothing.

"The fare is cheap and all can go"

Exhausted as if he has toted sack by sack
every pound of rock tunneled in the mountain
of racism & refusal;

"The rich and poor are there"

        & has borne 1
by 1 the body & soul of each of the 5
thousand students, faculty, & staff manning
Tuskegee's 161 buildings &
268 acres.

"No second class aboard this train"

Plip
Plop

"No dif-fer-ence in the fare"

". . . *occupied in some kind of labor."*

"Get on board little chil-dren, Get on
board, children,"

Strike!—Ring!
Strike!—Ring!

Plip
Plop.

—&,
as in dreams—
materializes—from
isn't
to
is!

Jim Crow—in a blue blaze haze with a Steam Drill
at his side, at his side, Lord, Steam Drill at his side.

"Get on board little children,

For there's room for ma-ny a ma-ny a more."

The challenge: "Going to keep you to the bottom till
you die . . ." unspoken but understood in bone &
corpuscles. Duel to the Death. "Get on board lit-
tle chil-dren, Get on board, children,"

Knows it's his last defense before his final
appraisement: his black name & place inscribed on the face
of eternal blackness, black as the nave of a
West Virginia mountain; black as the inside
of coal; cold black as black at the core of Jim Crow's
Black Codes.

Weary half smile as BT spits his palms, hums, "Raise 'em
up bullies and let 'em drop down, I'll beat you to
the bottom or die."

Jim Crow, cranking up his damned device, opines,
with a signifying, put-down-implying sneer,
"In trying to make it from 1 point to the next,
say equality for all coons, you're hexed. You've got
a willin' mind, but you'd just as well lay your sledge
aside, for, when I've hacked my separate but equal
track, no matter how hard you've tried, I'll be ahead
of all like you, & you'll still have more to do;
that last bumpy ½ way more to hammer through."

Chug-Thud!

Plip
Plop.

Cold stone, hot sweat, hellish funk of scorching steam, as
phosphorus sparks spit-hiss at spike-rings from
simultaneous steel on steel *CLINK* & *CHINK*

of metal stake on stone rung by his 9-pound hammer,
Lord, rung by his 9 pounds of man-swung steel.
(Christened Taliaferro, ironcutter, but
being, of necessity, as black men must, more
than his name — more — more — more-more-more-more-more-
    more.)
Staking the black heart of those multi-tons of
tectonic Pangaea crust's counteractions up-
thrust a million-million years before man, against
the backward suck, Crow's soul sieved by his puny hatreds,
oozed forth like pus.

"Jim Crow say to BT,
I'll load on more than you can stand . . ."

Strike! — Ring!
      Plip
Strike! — Ring!
      Plop
Strike! — Ring!
Chug — Thud!
      Sssssss
Chug — Thud!
      Sssssss
Chug — Thud!
Spray upon spray of skittered, lightning-bug blinkings,
freckling the countenance of the vast nought.
Chug — Thud!
Chug — Thud!
Chug — Thud!

Strike! — Ring!
Strike! — Ring!
Strike! — Ring!

In the air & reason-sucking scissure there is
no moon, sun, or clock, only the clangor-tongued
meter of their strike&chug & ring&thud
of every report of his hammer. Its purpose
& motive, stroke for stroke, records in each crack, rift,
lineament, chink, breach, rent, fissure, chap, gorge, slit, cut,
& frith tolling like End Time & Judgment Day.

"Jim Crow say to the nigger
I'll load more on you, more than you can stand,
More than you can stand.

"Nigger say to Jim Crow
load it, I'll stand it like a man,
yes, I'll stand it like a man."

Plip

Plop.

Stand it.
   Strike!—Ring!

   Chug—Thud!
Prove, beyond all odds,
   Strike!—Ring!

   Strike!—Ring!—
that it can be done—
   Chung—Thud!
That I can, without explanation, apology, or boast, do it—
   Strike!—Ring!—.
& break through to the light.
   Strike!—Ring!
   Strike!—Ring!
   Strike!—Ring!

Plop

"I am," they say together—
                    Strike!—
"The 1 of my time."
                    Thud!
"The spirit of my people."—
                    Ring!
Each indicating the other they quote Matthew
24:11: *"And many false prophets*
will arise and will mislead many."

Plip.
                    Chug—Thud!
                    Chug—Thud!
                    Chug—Thud!
                    Sssssssss ssss ss

Has he done enough?
                    Strike!—Ring!
More, he knows than any before him,
& his certainty spurs him on.
                    Strike—Ring!
& it spurs him on.

"Jim Crow say,
more than you can stand . . ."

I'll beat this steam drill of injustice down.
BT's
                    Strike!—Ring!
continues,
                    Strike!—Ring!
determined,
                    Strike!—Ring!
with less rapidity,

      Strike!—Ring!
but ricocheting
back & forward into the rock.

I'll beat Crow's racist steam drill down.
& from Crow's hot-air contraption an arrhythmic
          Thud! —— Chug-Chug—Thud!,
& offbeat Sssssss-hissing sigh as BT,
between his measured strikes listens above the draw
& neigh of his breathing, back through the thick maw
of humming silence—He hears Jim Crow's steam drill's
concussions & repercussions subsiding—farther
& farther back ——
              stutter with jerky wet wheezes & coughs.

A pause.

Then again,
weaker,
        Sssssss
             Sssssss
                sssssssofter each time . . .

"BT say to Jim Crow . . . ,"

           . . . then not at all . . .

". . . load it . . ."

Not believing for a moment Crow or his
apparatus are dead, but knowing in his time
he, BT, has weakened it. "The blows
I struck going to be the death of you, Lord, Lord,
now jump down spin around on that."
                Hearing in
answer Crow's murmurous minor-key caw as it

gathers itself, its rustle of wingfeathers &
scratch of claw its mute concession to having lost
the battle, but reminding of its tenacious
resolve to win the war.

Plip

BT's hammer heavy as his obligations to
& responsibilities for the multitudes
that he shepherds through bramble & 'cross the river,
yet hefts & hammers one last lick 'fore quittin' time,

"An' I'll beat Crow's steam drill of bias down,
Beat Crow's steam drill down."
                                        Strike!
". . . load it . . ."

& TAP & a whistling screech breaks through!

A twinkle of twilight . . .
& in white—*her.* Sunday morning sun of *Hope!*
Hallelujah. She smiles. *The reward of Loyalty*
& Trust. The rock on which to build our new prayer house!
"purge me . . . ," it's said in Psalms, "& I shall be clean;
wash me, & I shall be whiter than snow."

Hum hm h*mummm*

                    (but, just the other side of the light,
darkness, hears what he had not heard. But had. A
figure tap-tapping, taptapping, like darkness with-
in darkness. Stick & cur, yellow-gray, paw-nails click-
clicking with each guarding step; like some holy man,
in deep worn, down-home thread-bares, humming, welcoming . . .)

Hum hm h*mummm*

2-3
Hum hm huum*mummm*

plop
tip
tilt
topple . . .

"*. . . load it*
I'll stand it like a man . . ."

plop
tip
tilt
topple . . .

"*. . . Yes,*
I'll stand it
like a natural man . . ."

Sunday, November 15, 1915

NEGRO LEADER, DEAD

Founder of the Tuskegee Institute Expires

Dead, some say of "racial characteristics,"
meaning either high blood pressure or syphilis;
publically reported "Hardening of the arteries
following a nervous breakdown . . ."

Tuskegee endowed to the tune of nearly 2million.
Staff of 2hundred. 2hundred buildings, 1
hundred student built. Student population
2thousand.

Interlude
twelve

The Cock Crows Up a Dark Day.
Of a Pastoral Interlude.

Thursday, Nov. 18, 1915

From oak & morning mist, like phantoms forming in
silver emulsion, gray, work- & sun-aged figures
in their work & bluing-bleached sun-aged clothes, appear
into Tuskegee campus's chapel-like aura.

Stoic, mute silhouettes flocked against encircling
woods' panorama, witness official shuttling
& scurry of doers & dignitaries. Their
stately darkness, more defined now in warming light,
honoring the man, the occasion.

Dr. Carver, fighting to recall if he has
or has not completed some intended chore,
shuffles about with puzzled purpose, stopping mid-
task to whisk cotton fuzz from his dark, time-shined suit
with the light purple *Ruellia strepens* (wild
petunia) pinned on its lapel. The only
constant, his lips moving in silent prayer.

A viewing line 8,000 long is not recorded on film.

TR deeply grieves; praises BT for helping
bar shiftless Blacks from public office; praises him
for turning Negroes' minds from fruitless musings
on political advancement.
                    Theodore,
TR, "Teddy" Roosevelt, president by bullet
at 42, in a wish unfulfilled, succumbs
6 January, 1919, not in bright

battle, as was his fondest wish, but girded in
unspeakable grief from the year ago blow of
his youngest plunging Daedalus-like from the sky,
in a war the Bull Moose's bloodlust did not prompt.
10 days later cussed Prohibition kicks off.
As a tourist attraction, his & 3 others'
stony 60-foot-high mugs are blasted & hacked
into South Dakota's Black Hills on seized Native
land (Ain't it all?). Its design & construction
overseen by a card-carrying member of
the K.K.K. Dakota means "Alliance with
Friends."
   Ugh!

William Monroe Trotter, in 1934,
wearied to a frazzle by the spun-around
perceptions & distortions of his passion
for equality, will, in a final act of
single-minded discontent, on his 62d
birthday, spin around & jump down, from his roof,
to his death.

Interlude
thirteen

In Which Is Related a Visit to the Low Lands

See Tuskegee, Macon County Alabama farmland.

From across the creek the far-off shack looks to lean
the last way the wind blew. Crossed, closer: an old
colored man sits on its porch skirt.
                              Closer, enough
to speak. See the rusty-yellow hound at his feet,
alert on the glass-smooth dirt. Rib-thin as its master;
low growl, more threat than warning; nudged to hush by tap
of worn boot toe. Closer. Splintered guitar in his lap,
spidery fingers slide silent along the strings.
Hickory cane leans on his left, jar at his right.
Head tilts, ear cocked. Lids butterfly over pupils
color of clabbered milk. Forearms, neck, & temples
a roadmap of veiny brown highways. His hound, gaze
unwavering, watches.
                    As evening eases to
dark, says . . . Oh, there's been a heap—songs of work, women
loved; loved me; didn't. & loss— Like my boy— Still hardly,
hardly bear to call his name— The hound stirs, settles.
Did see to her, her & my grand getting way from
here.
        Fingertips stroke the strings light as Jesus
walking the water.
                    Was in them poplars, mile or
so yonder—
            Curls to fist.—Ashes—dust—

Down to the depot sometimes, short dog roll in, some-
body'd hunch me, say, There the principal is.
                                        Now
we all got freight to haul—same whether you the
pasture's big bull, or litter's littlest runt.

It's the song you carry eases the toting of
your load, keeps you from throwing up your hands, keeps deep
worrying from your mind—
                    Could hear in the tap-tap
of his walk, & rhythm when he'd talk was them
suitable old gospel hymns was his music; so
proper & white folks-appealing was too airy,
weariful, for full faith or trust to lead us
to leap screaming over in that raging, deep &
wide water divide between black & white; take our
chances to sink or swim.
                    Oh, his song tamed the willful,
the wayward out of him. So, he felt called to be
Moses, keep us sheep: bunched, baa, baa, baa, to bide, bide,
bide, down by the riverside, till our sweated blood
& tear-bleached fleece, appeased the bosses same as them
old bleated gospel hymns. & us pacified &
praying for faith or trust to shift the tide—while *our*
hope to reach & pluck the star of our choosing,
chars to ashes.
                    Somever, what this here music—
the weathered porch planks creak as he rocks—what-all these
blues'll do is allow you to face, & put right
your masks & feigns.

With the on-string mouse squeak of his calloused fingers,
the pat of his foot against the ground, the low growl
in the hound's throat, the gargle of ingested rage
& swallowed bile in his own, the distant train wail
he sings:

> *Oh, come along boys and line the track*
> (Hum hm h*mummm,)*
> *For the likes of him ain't comin' back,*
> (Hum hm h*mummm*
> *2-3)*

For the likes of him ain't never comin' back.
*(*Hum hm huum***mummm***
2-3
Hum hm huum***mummm.)*

Of Eulogies, in Which Mrs. Wells
& Mr. Du Bois Have the Final Word

Ida B., scrappy as a peckerwood's feist, says,
"Somebody must show that the Afro-American
race is more sinned against than sinning, and it seems
to have fallen upon me to do so," & takes
her life in her hands, doing what men don't or won't
or can't. Her name is 'buked & scorned. She stands, says
they're not dangled from limbs like yuletide baubles
because they're renegades like that photo-play Gus,
nor for panting after white women like half-cast
Stoneman (both blackened-faced whitemen). She says they're hung
to cover their killer's gory greed & guilts.

W.E.B. eulogizes BT
as sincere but wrong, goes from there finding his voice
& way on his own, led by evolving insights
& disillusionments. He defies & decamps.
Can't keep a friend: Trotter, Wilson, Walter White,
Roy Wilkins, NAACP, Marcus Garvey.
Is prone to flattery. Dies in Accra, Ghana
on 27 August, 1963.

He is 95. The next day Martin Luther King
sings his dream at the March on Washington.

& they come to order as the up beat down beat
strikes up the band, & the rich get richer, the poor
need more, 2, THREE, 4 & Time & the Press & Church
& State & the American populace
consumers, the Americanists Forward March,
as the band plays on.

They don't come by ones . . .

Hum hm h*mummm*
2-3
Hum hm huum***mummm***

After Words

It will be difficult for me not to "make sport for the Philistines" by pulling down a house or two; since, when I once take pen in hand, I must say what comes uppermost, or fling it away.

—Lord Byron (1788–1824), English poet, letter to publisher John Murray, 6 June 1822 (published in Byron's *Letters and Journals,* vol. 9, ed. Leslie A. Marchand, 1979)

Quote: "lit a lantern in the bright morning hours." Has he got lost? asks one. Did he lose his way like a child? asks another. Or is he hiding? Is he afraid of us?

—Friedrich Wilhelm Nietzsche (1844–1900), "Parable of the Madman" (1882, 1887)

"Tut, tut, child! Everything's got a moral, if only you can find it."

—The Duchess, in *Alice in Wonderland,* by Lewis Carroll (1865)

One is astonished in the study of history at the recurrence of the idea that evil must be forgotten, distorted, skimmed over. We must not remember that Daniel Webster got drunk but only remember that he was a splendid constitutional lawyer. We must forget that George Washington was a slave owner . . . and simply remember the things we regard as creditable and inspiring. The difficulty, of course, with this philosophy is that history loses its value as an incentive and example; it paints perfect men and noble nations, but it does not tell the truth.

—W.E.B. Du Bois (1868–1963),
"Black Reconstruction in America, 1860–1880" (1935)